The Essential Poets

❖❖

Volume 1   The Essential Keats*

Volume 2   The Essential Whitman

Volume 3   The Essential Melville

Volume 4   The Essential Blake*

Volume 5   The Essential Herbert

Volume 6   The Essential Wordsworth

Volume 7   The Essential Campion

Volume 8   The Essential Donne*

Volume 9   The Essential Byron*

Volume 10   The Essential Wyatt

Volume 11   The Essential Burns

Volume 12   The Essential Rossetti

Volume 13   The Essential Browning

*BOOK/CASSETTE PACKAGES AVAILABLE

The Essential Rossetti

❖❖

Dante Gabriel Rossetti

BORN 12 MAY 1828
DIED 9 APRIL 1882

The Essential
ROSSETTI

Selected and with an
Introduction by

JOHN HOLLANDER

The Ecco Press
New York

Introduction and selection copyright © 1985, 1989 by John Hollander
Published in 1990 by The Ecco Press
26 West 17th Street, New York, N.Y. 10011
Published simultaneously in Canada by
Penguin Books Canada Ltd., Ontario
Printed in the United States of America
Designed by Reg Perry

FIRST EDITION

Library of Congress Cataloging-in-Publication Data
Rossetti, Dante Gabriel, 1828–1882.
[Poems. Selections]
The essential Rossetti / selected and with an introduction by John Hollander.
p. cm.—(The Essential poets; v. 13)
Two poems translated from Italian.
I. Hollander, John. II. Title.
III. Series: Essential poets (New York, N.Y.); v. 13.
PR5242.H65   1990   88-27314 CIP
821'.8—dc19

ISBN 0-88001-196-3

Portrait of Dante Gabriel Rossetti
by W. Holman Hunt
Courtesy of the City Art Gallery,
Manchester, England

Cassette recordings of live readings and interviews with
several of the series editors are available directly from
The Ecco Press in handsome book/cassette packages for $15.95
each. Call or write for details. Published by arrangement
with The Listening Library, Old Greenwich, CT. Jason Shinder,
general series interviewer and executive producer, is the
founder and director of The Writers' Voice, New York City.

Contents

❖❖

INTRODUCTION BY JOHN HOLLANDER   3

POEMS   17

The Blessed Damozel   17

Jenny   22

Love's Nocturn   35

The House of Life: A Sonnet-Sequence   41

Eden Bower   93

The Stream's Secret   100

My Sister's Sleep   108

For an Annunciation   111

The Portrait   111

For Our Lady of the Rocks   115

At the Sun-rise in 1848   116

A Trip to Paris and Belgium   116

For a Venetian Pastoral   137

For an Allegorical Dance of Women   137

For "Ruggiero and Angelica"   138

For a Virgin and Child   139

For a Marriage of St. Catherine   140

The Sea-Limits   141

The Mirror   142

During Music   142

Penumbra   143

Words on the Window-pane   144

A Match with the Moon   145

Sudden Light   145

Dawn on the Night-Journey   146

The Woodspurge   146

Venus Verticordia   147

A Sea-Spell   148

Troy Town   148

A Death-Parting   152

For Spring   153

For the Holy Family   153

"Found"   154

The Orchard-Pit   155

TRANSLATIONS   156

Sestina   156

The Ballad of Dead Ladies   157

ABOUT THE EDITOR   159

For Cristina Giorcelli
. . . non rifiutando i luoghi dove eravamo stati prima
Ma portando una parte di ciò fu in ciò che sarà.

The Essential Rossetti

❖

Introduction

❖

It is well over a hundred years since the death of Dante Gabriel Rossetti, and for something like the last sixty of these he has been, like his younger friend Swinburne, a remarkably underrated poet. This critical neglect was in some measure the result of the antiromantic stance of Anglo-American literary modernism. William Butler Yeats acknowledged Rossetti's role as a "subconscious influence" on the following generation, but it is still startling for modern readers to hear his voice lurking in those canonical modernists Eliot, Pound, and Frost. (Few know, I believe, that Rossetti found, meditated upon, and was struck by the passage from Petronius's *Satyricon* that Eliot later used as the final epigraph for *The Waste Land,* for example.) It was precisely Yeats's supposedly utter repudiation of the old adornments of that following generation—his own—in favor of "walking naked" that remains a central myth of modernist literary history. And yet how much of that nakedness is to be found in some of Rossetti's poems is still surprising. Ezra Pound praised Rossetti, early on, as a translator who made available medieval materials before Pound's own modernist medievalism—presumably more tough-minded—had treated them suitably. But certainly Rossetti's very great sestina, translated from Dante Alighieri's *"Al poco giorno ed al gran cerchio d'ombra,"* with its ringing concluding stanzas

> Yet shall the streams turn back and climb the hills
> Before Love's flame in this damp wood and green
> Burn, as it burns within a youthful lady,
> For my sake, who would sleep away in stone

| 3 |

> My life, or feed like beasts upon the grass,
> Only to see her garments cast a shade.
>
> How dark soe'er the hills throw out their shade,
> Under her summer-green the beautiful lady
> Covers it, like a stone covered in grass.

is more powerful than any of Pound's versions of the poetry of Guido Cavalcanti.

We can observe that Rossetti's discovery of perfect end-words—those crucial recurring elements of the sestina form—for the Italian ones uncannily also allows analogous phonological relations to flourish among them. "Shade," "hills," "grass," "green," "stone," "lady" (in the order in which they appear in the first stanza) perfectly translate *ombra, colli, erba, verde, pietra, donna.* But they mirror the internal affinities of the original words: *om*bra–*don*na (*sh*ade–*la*dy) for example, and *er*ba–*ver*de (here the assonance is picked up by the alliterative *gr*ass–*gr*een). Similarly, the syntactic boldness, in the lines quoted above, of "would sleep away in stone / My life" (for *"che mi torrei dormire in pietra / Tutto il mio tempo"*) uses the enjambment to distance the deferred object from the verb even more, and imply that the "in stone" is part of the verb "sleep" itself. This is a Miltonic stroke, even as is what the rhetoricians call the tmesis of the syntax of "this damp wood and green" (for *"questo legno molle e verde,"* where that same construction usually found in Italian poetry is absent): Rossetti could easily have written "this wood damp and green," but preferred, in a more intense mode, to remind one of the Italian grammar and at the same time conduct the reader through the two orders of predication in the case of the wood, emerging after the fact of the dampness into the returning, refrainlike terminal word "green" (as if to say, "this damp wood and—yes, here we go again—green"). But wherever one looks at Dante's original, one marvels at both the fidelity and the beauty, supposedly incompatible in translation, of what is an astonishing English poem of its own.

Pound writes of Rossetti, whether in blame or praise, as if the latter were nothing but a stylist and a literary historian from whom some good things could be learned and some bad ones avoided. Pound writes as if imagination were only rhetorical ingenuity, as if the substance of poetry and its mythologies of love and death, self and other, quest and loss, existed only in the diseases of bad critical discourse. But the essence of what Pound is blind to in his work Rossetti reveals, brilliantly and darkly at once, in a miniature *ars poetica,* a poem of poetic craft. The prefatory sonnet written in 1880 to introduce his major poetic work, *The House of Life,* at first glance purports to deal merely with the sonnet form itself:

> *A Sonnet is a moment's monument,—*
> > *Memorial from the Soul's eternity*
> > *To one dead deathless hour. Look that it be,*
> *Whether for lustral rite or dire portent,*
> *Of its own arduous fulness reverent:*
> > *Carve it in ivory or in ebony,*
> > *As Day or Night may rule; and let Time see*
> *Its flowering crest impearled and orient.*
>
> *A Sonnet is a coin: its face reveals*
> > *The Soul,—its converse, to what Power't is due:—*
> *Whether for tribute to the august appeals*
> > *Of Life, or dower in Love's high retinue,*
> *It serve; or, 'mid the dark wharf's cavernous breath,*
> *In Charon's palm it pay the toll to Death.*

But this is more than merely an exercise in a genre—the "sonnet-on-the-sonnet"—continued from Wordsworth and Keats. Rossetti's "moment's monument" is the monument *of,* or produced by, a moment's vision and work and also the monument *to* the very brevity of that moment: Rossetti's sonnet is always, no matter what its putative "subject," the cry of its own occasion. The sculptural fable of art and life is revised from that of a freestanding figure, in the octave, down to the carved relief of a coin, in the self-characterizing sestet. It is an antique coin, still of great value; but as with all ancient coins, the matter of payment for the Stygian ferry creeps into the accounting as it does in Rossetti's closing, his bottom line, as it were, which reveals what had been implicit among the other transactions—with Life and Love—all along. This sonnet, conspicuously reverent "of its own arduous fullness," is about poetry altogether. The epigraph to the sonnet sequence *The House of Life*—itself a discontinuous frieze of moments' monuments—is thus a reminder of final costs, of the way in which the whole procession of life itself is always being viewed with an averted gaze.

In its central concern for human meaning, for the existential role of fable in our lives, the miniature bas-relief of Rossetti's coin (cut by the hand of the artist, caressed as art by the hand of the antiquary, passed on from hand to hand in ancient trade) thus constitutes a monument more significant and more mighty than the guarded, scaled-down decorations, the enamels and cameos that Pound and Eliot adapted from the French poet Théophile Gautier. The painter-poet's late romantic half-personifications of Life and Death were far less attractive to subsequent twentieth-century poetry than the dismantled figurines of irony and pity of the later poet-as-sculptor. Once the modern reader can penetrate a high, post-Keatsian gesture, Rossetti's poetry will be felt not as "Pre-Raphaelite" but rather as tough, creatively problematic, rejecting easy or fake answers to ultimate questions, masterfully coping with the central modern problem of treating the great in the small. Indeed, if Rossetti's poems seem sweetmeats to a reserved, modernist taste, there is yet a hard nut to crack within, whereas Pound's poetic rhetoric is like a candy with a hard surface which quickly melts away to the fudge within.

The whole of *The House of Life* is problematic in several ways; both its title (an astrological trope? a more general postbiblical figure of a consecrated space? a place *in, made of, belonging to, dedicated to,* etc. Life?) and its very lack of sequentiality are hard to deal with. This is more like an anthology of sonnets, written over a thirty-year period, brooding on eros and art, lit by the flaming presences of three female personages—a Beata Beatrix out of Dante, a Proserpina-Pandora figure, and a Lilith, these last two being pure Dante Gabriel, and in whom we may discern reflections of, respectively, Elizabeth Siddal, the poet's wife, a suicide in 1862; Jane (Mrs. William) Morris, and Rossetti's model and housekeeper, Fanny Cornforth. The poems range from the direct and naturalistic to the highly and manifestly allegorical, from the postcoital bed of "Nuptial Sleep" or the nature poetry of "Barren Spring" or "Autumn Idleness" ("The deer gaze calling, dappled white and dun, / As if, being foresters of old, the sun / Had marked them with the shade of forest-leaves" sounds, as Rossetti does often, like Robert Frost), where the hidden allegory is almost Emersonian, to poems like "Passion and Worship." Here, a pair of personifications that might easily have come from the early Italian poets are reinforced by a traditional neoclassical distinction between the qualities of their musical attributes. Passion has a wind instrument, Worship a string; the particular harp and archaically designated "hautboy" are importations from pictorial iconography:

> One flame-winged brought a white-winged harp-player
>   Even where my lady and I lay all alone;
>   Saying: "Behold, this minstrel is unknown;
> Bid him depart, for I am minstrel here:
> Only my strains are to Love's dear ones dear."
>   Then said I: "Though thine hautboy's rapturous tone
>   Unto my lady still this harp makes moan,
> And still she deems the cadence deep and clear."
>
> Then said my lady: "Thou art Passion of Love,
>   And this Love's Worship: both he plights to me.

> *Thy mastering music walks the sunlit sea:*
> *But where wan water trembles in the grove*
> *And the wan moon is all the light thereof,*
>   *This harp still makes my name its voluntary."*

While "wan music trembles in the grove" is a fine visual correlative for the acoustic actualities of harp music, the sound of an early oboe, which Rossetti had probably never heard, is so thin and nasal and even braying that the instrument's role is purely emblematic. From classical times on, the wind–string distinction has corresponded to the contraries of energy and reason, will and wit (in Elizabethan terminology), Dionysian and Apollonian. Rossetti's pictorializing of the musical sound is effective in the case of the string music of Love's white messenger; the word "hautboy," on the other hand, is purely iconographic.

Even more abstractly so is the celebrated image of the monochord, in the sonnet of the same name, which amused Swinburne, and which William Michael Rossetti, in his notes to the edition of 1911, sought to dissolve completely from the poem, by arguing that the name of the archaic instrument alone, the word itself, invoked "an unspeakably mysterious bond between the universe and the soul of man." Originally published as a separate sonnet of 1870 called "Written During Music," the poem began: "Is it the moved air or the moving sound / That is Life's self and draws my life from me." When included in *The House of Life*, the first line was rewritten and the octave went as follows:

> *Is it this sky's vast vault or ocean's sound*
>   *That is Life's self and draws my life from me,*
>   *And by instinct ineffable decree*
> *Holds my breath quailing on the bitter bound?*
> *Nay, is it Life or Death, thus thunder-crown'd,*
>   *That 'mid the tide of all emergency*
>   *Now notes my separate wave, and to what sea*
> *Its difficult eddies labour in the ground?*

Even though the symbol of the archaic, largely didactic, instrument is retained in the title, the musical context has indeed vanished.

Rossetti was so much more capable of being overwhelmed by the poetic power of great art than were most nineteenth-century critics (save, of course, John Ruskin and Walter Pater) that he was unable, in his own painting, to transcend illustration to the degree that the major painters associated with the Pre-Raphaelite Brotherhood were (Ford Madox Brown, the best, and, before he went to the bad, John Everett Millais). His canvases have come in time to assume the true color of their provinciality, of their earnest half-amateurishness. Even a return to trivial but profitable favor, and mindless, tasteless judgment in the contemporary art market of figurative illustration will not do much for the stature of Rossetti's painting. Not so for the poems; they look better every year. Aside from the central canon of his work—*The House of Life,* the sonnets for pictures, "The Stream's Secret," "Jenny," "The Sea-Limits," "Sudden Light," "Love's Nocturn," "Eden Bower," "Troy Town," "The Orchard Pit," fragmentary as it is—there are such poems as that splendid short lyric "The Woodspurge," whose poetic "action" is that of a radical reconstruction of an available emblem into a far more powerful metaphor. The speaker, grief-stricken in a bleak windy outdoor scene, collapses forward in despair ("My hair was over in the grass, / My naked ears heard the day pass"—which is poetic language astonishing enough in itself). But then

> *My eyes, wide open, had the run*
> *Of some ten weeds to fix upon;*
> *Among these few, out of the sun,*
> *The woodspurge flowered, three cups in one.*

> *From perfect grief there need not be*
> *Wisdom or even memory:*
> *One thing then learnt remains to me,—*
> *The woodspurge has a cup of three.*

The flower is claimed here by no iconographic fancy: there is no trinitarian device, no allusion to ideal triads, lurking here. The *thisness,* as Gerard Manley Hopkins might have had it, of this unique perception of the wild flower's structure at that moment outlasts, for the speaker, any moralization of his own feelings. The epistemological moral only is left, which the reader, doing his own poetic work, must go on to draw. "The Woodspurge" not only embodies a Joycean epiphany, in which "a sudden light transfigures a trivial thing" (as Pater, mediating between Rossetti and Joyce, was to put it), but also unfolds the very action of a modern short story (from *Dubliners,* say) in miniature.

This prematurely modernist mode in Rossetti is frequently accompanied by a tone, diction, and rhythm that are far more direct and colloquial than those of the high rhetoric of poems like *The House of Life.* Consider that—for me—strangely charming sonnet called "A Match with the Moon":

> Weary already, weary miles to-night
>   I walked for bed: and so, to get some ease,
>   I dogged the flying moon with similes.
> And like a wisp she doubled on my sight
> In ponds; and caught in tree-tops like a kite;
>   And in a globe of film all liquorish
>   Swam full-faced like a silly silver fish;—
> Last like a bubble shot the welkin's height
> Where my road turned, and got behind me, and sent
>   My wizened shadow craning round at me,
>   And jeered, "So, step the measure,—one two three!"
> And if I faced on her, looked innocent.
> But just at parting, halfway down a dell,
> She kissed me for good-night. So you'll not tell.

The first seven lines and the last three are, once again, almost pure Robert Frost, the last one astonishingly so. This is, of course, to say how much Rossetti Frost had absorbed quite early on, but it is also to point out how misunderstood is the received view of Rossetti's language among those who haven't reread him. That he was an erotic poet who suffered the attack of a prudish fool named Buchanan is well-known; but that he was a direct poet of nature has been largely forgotten. Even in some of his earliest poems, Rossetti can render with a potent and even astonishing precision the effects of natural sound—and, even more remarkably, urban and industrial noise—both within and upon the landscape in which the sounds arise. Consider, for example, that remarkable and remarkably unappreciated series of poems written on the train journey that he and Holman Hunt took to France and Belgium in 1849. *A Trip to Paris and Belgium* (sent to his brother, William Michael) combines blank-verse journal and epistle with sonnets and a few inset lyrics, the first covering the travel by rail between London and Bruges, and the rhymed poems largely recording and commemorating stops and places. The handling of landscape moving by outside a train window is brilliant throughout these poems (the sequence opens, in "London to Folkstone," with "A constant keeping-past of shaken trees, / And a bewildered glitter of loose road"); the silent film unrolling alongside the train begins to be underscored with the audible only when the elements of the landscape themselves register the noise of the passing engine and cars:

> *And, seen through fences or a bridge far off,*
> *Trees that in moving keep their intervals*
> *Still one 'twixt bar and bar; and then at times*
> *Long reaches of green level, where one cow,*
> *Feeding among her fellows that feed on,*
> *Lifts her slow neck, and gazes for the sound.*

Later, passing into open country from between brick walls, he registers the "short gathered champing of pent sound," and even seems to feel, "close about the face / A wind of noise that is along like God." Still further on, in the sonnet "In the Train, and at Versailles," he registers the onset of silence after the noise of travel as something palpably filling the room of the landscape:

> . . . . *A great silence here,*
> *Through the long planted alleys, to the long*
> *Distance of water. More than tune or song,*
> *Silence shall grow to awe within thine eyes,*
> *Till thy thought swim with the blue turning sphere.*

In "On the Road," a subsequent blank-verse section, the very silence itself is audible: "A dead pause then / With giddy humming silence in the cars"; some lines later in the same poem, the traveler reports "A heavy clamour that fills up the brain / Like thought grown burdensome; and in the ears / Speed that seems striving to o'ertake itself." The first of these clauses might perhaps remind us that Rossetti was indeed carrying Browning (at least *Sordello*) with him on this trip; the second is a representation that seems more of the 1920s.

The finest section of the sequence is "Antwerp to Ghent," and in it the blanketing effect of the droning, continuing noise of the train on other sounds is wonderfully portrayed:

> *The darkness is a tumult. We tear on,*
> *The roll behind us and the cry before,*
> *Constantly, in a lull of intense speed*
> *And thunder. Any other sound is known*
> *Merely by sight.*

The casual, often conversational, journal-entry quality of the blank verse (I have discussed elsewhere how lines like "Our speed is such the sparks our engine leaves / Are burning after the whole train has passed" remind one of the blank verse of Frost's eclogues) give these observations the virtues of the pencil, rather than of the more resonant brush.

In contrast with the naturally visual realm of these epistolary blank-verse passages, the purely visionary demesne of a poem like "Love's Nocturn" draws upon medievalized mythology, which it then revises. This mysterious and difficult poem about erotic dreaming is in the form of an office of Love (the title suggests the liturgical term, rather than the name of the musical composition first used by John Field) as the god of dreams. At the outset he is invoked as "Master of the murmuring courts / Where the shapes of sleep convene," and the poem itself starts out in a region of consciousness in which sight and hearing begin to dissolve into each other in sleep. The poet petitions Love to send his sleeping lady a dream of himself, and in a later stanza introduces the role that audition, rather than vision, will play:

> Master, is it soothly said
>   That, as echoes of man's speech
> Far in secret clefts are made,
>   So do all men's bodies reach
>   Shadows o'er thy sunken beach,—
>   Shape or shade
>   In those halls pourtrayed of each?

An old myth of echo becomes eroticized both in image and in function here, as parallel to the shadows of projected desire that exist as every man's double in Love's dream kingdom. It is this benign *Doppelgänger* the poet hopes to meet—"Groping in the windy stair, / (Darkness and the breath of space / Like loud waters everywhere,)"—and send into the sleep of his lady. But it is in sound rather than in sight or in dreamed touch that his "body's phantom" is to come to her:

> Where in groves the gracile Spring
>   Trembles, with mute orison
> Confidently strengthening,
>   Water's voice and wind's as one
>   Shed an echo in the sun.

With this near-Clevelandism of romantic imagery the blended voices of the *locus amoenus* figure also the mingling of shadow and echo, sight and sound. The poet's emanation continues to sing to her in the two musical modalities of absence and presence, longing and fulfillment:

> *Soft as Spring,*
> *Master, bid it sing and moan.*

> *Song shall tell how glad and strong*
> *Is the night she soothes alway;*
> *Moan shall grieve with that parched tongue*
> *Of the brazen hours of day:*
> *Sounds as of the springtide they,*
> *Moan and song,*
> *While the chill months long for May.*

Both of these melodies, the tones of song and of moan, are ultimately Keatsian (e.g., the "parched tongue"), as is the overall movement toward the usurpation of vision's kingdom by hearing. It is the specifically erotic milieu that is Rossetti's characteristic one. Even the Romantic cliché of the Aeolian harp—not as the strong Coleridgean or Shelleyan emblem of inspiration and imaginative response, but as the languid image of nature reclaiming the suspended or abandoned instrument, a most ubiquitous trope—becomes a figure for relinquished desire. Toward the end of the poem, the speaker tells Love that if his lady's dreaming world is already occupied by another's shadow of desire, then his own must withdraw:

> *Like a vapour wan and mute,*
> *Like a flame, so let it pass;*
> *One low sigh across her lute,*
> *One dull breath against her glass.*

The "lute" is a purely visionary instrument, figuratively the lady's heart, abandoned and inaccessible as his instrument now. Any stringed instrument would do for the sigh across it, and the particular archaism here is part of the apparatus of the poem that is so redolent of the medieval Italian poetry he had already translated.

One of Rossetti's most uniquely transformed genres is what scholars call poetic ecphrasis, the kind of poem that addresses a particular and actual work of art (rather than a notional one, like Homer's shield of Achilles, or the tapestries in Book III of *The Faerie Queene*), the speaking pictures of verse giving voice, as it were, to the mute poetry of painting. Poetic language confronts the pictorial Other in an erotic or agonistic way, and imagines by interpreting. Ecphrastic poems (all too frequently on paintings by Pieter Brueghel the Elder) abound in most books of verse written in the past decade, but it was Rossetti who propounded the modern agenda for pictorial poems in English, long before the canonical anthology-pieces by Rilke and Auden made the genre seem a modernist invention. Certain sections of *The House of Life* written for, and to, his own paintings aside, Rossetti produced some twenty-six poems—almost all of them sonnets—for paintings by Renaissance and later artists. The greatest of these is the sonnet to Leonardo da Vinci's *Virgin of the Rocks* (the version of the painting in London), with its rocks, caves, and shades of death; its foreground figures of Mary, her son, and the infant St. John, attended by the angel Gabriel; and its background caves opening out through close passages to distant, shining water. Rossetti's poem confronts the paradoxes of life and death, of entrances and exits, inherent in the scene's darknesses. Its own structures of questioning octave and answering sestet, both commencing with the word "Mother," trope the relation of foreground and background in the picture, and the difficult "pass" invoked in the ninth line (which sounds so much like Eliot's "Ash-Wednesday") points to a poetic passage— what Harold Bloom would call a "poetic crossing"—as well. It is significant too that the angel Gabriel is missing from the ecphrastic account, as if Dante Gabriel were replacing him as shower and teller. Almost as strong is the sonnet on the *Concert Champêtre* in the Louvre (then thought to be by Giorgione alone), a poem on which Pater so obviously drew for his celebrated meditation on the same painting in *The Renaissance*. But whether giving readings of pictures by Botticelli, Mantegna, Memling, Ingres, or Burne-Jones, or even some unspecified words on a windowpane, Rossetti's questioning gaze into the depths of art pierces always through to the heart of life.

This selection contains all of Rossetti's major poetry, including ecphrastic sonnets just described, ballads, *The House of Life* complete, the whole of *A Trip to Paris and Belgium* (never before reprinted), and a wealth of others. I have used the texts and ordering of the revised and enlarged posthumous edition by the poet's brother, William Michael Rossetti (London, 1911), even though this may not have been the author's own finally intended sequence.

—JOHN HOLLANDER

Poems

The Blessed Damozel

The blessed damozel leaned out
   From the gold bar of Heaven;
Her eyes were deeper than the depth
   Of waters stilled at even;
She had three lilies in her hand,
   And the stars in her hair were seven.

Her robe, ungirt from clasp to hem,
   No wrought flowers did adorn,
But a white rose of Mary's gift,
   For service meetly worn;
Her hair that lay along her back
   Was yellow like ripe corn.

Herseemed she scarce had been a day
   One of God's choristers;
The wonder was not yet quite gone
   From that still look of hers;
Albeit, to them she left, her day
   Had counted as ten years.

(To one, it is ten years of years.
   . . . Yet now, and in this place,
Surely she leaned o'er me—her hair
   Fell all about my face . . .

Nothing: the autumn-fall of leaves.
    The whole year sets apace.)

It was the rampart of God's house
    That she was standing on;
By God built over the sheer depth
    The which is Space begun;
So high, that looking downward thence
    She scarce could see the sun.

It lies in Heaven, across the flood
    Of ether, as a bridge.
Beneath, the tides of day and night
    With flame and darkness ridge
The void, as low as where this earth
    Spins like a fretful midge.

Around her, lovers, newly met
    'Mid deathless love's acclaims,
Spoke evermore among themselves
    Their heart-remembered names;
And the souls mounting up to God
    Went by her like thin flames.

And still she bowed herself and stooped
    Out of the circling charm;
Until her bosom must have made
    The bar she leaned on warm,
And the lilies lay as if asleep
    Along her bended arm.

From the fixed place of Heaven she saw
    Time like a pulse shake fierce
Through all the worlds. Her gaze still strove

Within the gulf to pierce
Its path; and now she spoke as when
    The stars sang in their spheres.

The sun was gone now; the curled moon
    Was like a little feather
Fluttering far down the gulf; and now
    She spoke through the still weather.
Her voice was like the voice the stars
    Had when they sang together.

(Ah sweet! Even now, in that bird's song,
    Strove not her accents there,
Fain to be hearkened? When those bells
    Possessed the mid-day air,
Strove not her steps to reach my side
    Down all the echoing stair?)

"I wish that he were come to me,
    For he will come," she said.
"Have I not prayed in Heaven?—on earth,
    Lord, Lord, has he not pray'd?
Are not two prayers a perfect strength?
    And shall I feel afraid?

"When round his head the aureole clings,
    And he is clothed in white,
I'll take his hand and go with him
    To the deep wells of light;
As unto a stream we will step down,
    And bathe there in God's sight.

"We two will stand beside that shrine,
    Occult, withheld, untrod,

Whose lamps are stirred continually
    With prayer sent up to God;
And see our old prayers, granted, melt
    Each like a little cloud.

"We two will lie i' the shadow of
    That living mystic tree
Within whose secret growth the Dove
    Is sometimes felt to be,
While every leaf that His plumes touch
    Saith His Name audibly.

"And I myself will teach to him,
    I myself, lying so,
The songs I sing here; which his voice
    Shall pause in, hushed and slow,
And find some knowledge at each pause,
    Or some new thing to know."

(Alas! we two, we two, thou say'st!
    Yea, one wast thou with me
That once of old. But shall God lift
    To endless unity
The soul whose likeness with thy soul
    Was but its love for thee?)

"We two," she said, "will seek the groves
    Where the lady Mary is,
With her five handmaidens, whose names
    Are five sweet symphonies,
Cecily, Gertrude, Magdalen,
    Margaret and Rosalys.

"Circlewise sit they, with bound locks
    And foreheads garlanded;
Into the fine cloth white like flame
    Weaving the golden thread,
To fashion the birth-robes for them
    Who are just born, being dead.

"He shall fear, haply, and be dumb:
    Then will I lay my cheek
To his, and tell about our love,
    Not once abashed or weak:
And the dear Mother will approve
    My pride, and let me speak.

"Herself shall bring us, hand in hand,
    To Him round whom all souls
Kneel, the clear-ranged unnumbered heads
    Bowed with their aureoles:
And angels meeting us shall sing
    To their citherns and citoles.

"There will I ask of Christ the Lord
    Thus much for him and me:—
Only to live as once on earth
    With Love,—only to be,
As then awhile, for ever now
    Together, I and he."

She gazed and listened and then said,
    Less sad of speech than mild,—
"All this is when he comes." She ceased.
    The light thrilled towards her, fill'd
With angels in strong level flight.
    Her eyes prayed, and she smil'd.

(I saw her smile.) But soon their path
    Was vague in distant spheres:
And then she cast her arms along
    The golden barriers,
And laid her face between her hands,
    And wept. (I heard her tears.)

Jenny

Vengeance of Jenny's case! Fie on her! Never name her, child!—(Mrs. Quickly.)

Lazy laughing languid Jenny,
Fond of a kiss and fond of a guinea,
Whose head upon my knee to-night
Rests for a while, as if grown light
With all our dances and the sound
To which the wild tunes spun you round:
Fair Jenny mine, the thoughtless queen
Of kisses which the blush between
Could hardly make much daintier;
Whose eyes are as blue skies, whose hair
Is countless gold incomparable:
Fresh flower, scarce touched with signs that tell
Of Love's exuberant hotbed:—Nay,
Poor flower left torn since yesterday
Until to-morrow leave you bare;
Poor handful of bright spring-water
Flung in the whirlpool's shrieking face;
Poor shameful Jenny, full of grace
Thus with your head upon my knee;—
Whose person or whose purse may be
The lodestar of your reverie?

This room of yours, my Jenny, looks
A change from mine so full of books,
Whose serried ranks hold fast, forsooth,
So many captive hours of youth,—
The hours they thieve from day and night
To make one's cherished work come right,
And leave it wrong for all their theft,
Even as to-night my work was left:
Until I vowed that since my brain
And eyes of dancing seemed so fain,
My feet should have some dancing too:—
And thus it was I met with you.
Well, I suppose 'twas hard to part,
For here I am. And now, sweetheart,
You seem too tired to get to bed.

It was a careless life I led
When rooms like this were scarce so strange
Not long ago. What breeds the change,—
The many aims or the few years?
Because to-night it all appears
Something I do not know again.

The cloud's not danced out of my brain—
The cloud that made it turn and swim
While hour by hour the books grew dim.
Why, Jenny, as I watch you there,—
For all your wealth of loosened hair,
Your silk ungirdled and unlac'd
And warm sweets open to the waist,
All golden in the lamplight's gleam,—
You know not what a book you seem,
Half-read by lightning in a dream!
How should you know, my Jenny? Nay,

And I should be ashamed to say:—
Poor beauty, so well worth a kiss!
But while my thought runs on like this
With wasteful whims more than enough,
I wonder what you're thinking of.

    If of myself you think at all,
What is the thought?—conjectural
On sorry matters best unsolved?—
Or inly is each grace revolved
To fit me with a lure?—or (sad
To think!) perhaps you're merely glad
That I'm not drunk or ruffianly
And let you rest upon my knee.

    For sometimes, were the truth confess'd,
You're thankful for a little rest,—
Glad from the crush to rest within,
From the heart-sickness and the din
Where envy's voice at virtue's pitch
Mocks you because your gown is rich;
And from the pale girl's dumb rebuke,
Whose ill-clad grace and toil-worn look
Proclaim the strength that keeps her weak,
And other nights than yours bespeak;
And from the wise unchildish elf,
To schoolmate lesser than himself
Pointing you out, what thing you are:—
Yes, from the daily jeer and jar,
From shame and shame's outbraving too,
Is rest not sometimes sweet to you?—
But most from the hatefulness of man,
Who spares not to end what he began,
Whose acts are ill and his speech ill,

Who, having used you at his will,
Thrusts you aside, as when I dine
I serve the dishes and the wine.

Well, handsome Jenny mine, sit up:
I've filled our glasses, let us sup,
And do not let me think of you,
Lest shame of yours suffice for two.
What, still so tired? Well, well then, keep
Your head there, so you do not sleep;
But that the weariness may pass
And leave you merry, take this glass.
Ah! lazy lily hand, more bless'd
If ne'er in rings it had been dress'd
Nor ever by a glove conceal'd!

Behold the lilies of the field,
They toil not neither do they spin;
(So doth the ancient text begin,—
Not of such rest as one of these
Can share.) Another rest and ease
Along each summer-sated path
From its new lord the garden hath,
Than that whose spring in blessings ran
Which praised the bounteous husbandman,
Ere yet, in days of hankering breath,
The lilies sickened unto death.

What, Jenny, are your lilies dead?
Aye, and the snow-white leaves are spread
Like winter on the garden-bed.
But you had roses left in May,—
They were not gone too. Jenny, nay,
But must your roses die, and those

Their purfled buds that should unclose?
Even so; the leaves are curled apart,
Still red as from the broken heart,
And here's the naked stem of thorns.

Nay, nay, mere words. Here nothing warns
As yet of winter. Sickness here
Or want alone could waken fear,—
Nothing but passion wrings a tear.
Except when there may rise unsought
Haply at times a passing thought
Of the old days which seem to be
Much older than any history
That is written in any book;
When she would lie in fields and look
Along the ground through the blown grass
And wonder where the city was,
Far out of sight, whose broil and bale
They told her then for a child's tale.

Jenny, you know the city now.
A child can tell the tale there, how
Some things which are not yet enroll'd
In market-lists are bought and sold
Even till the early Sunday light,
When Saturday night is market-night
Everywhere, be it dry or wet,
And market-night in the Haymarket.
Our learned London children know,
Poor Jenny, all your pride and woe;
Have seen your lifted silken skirt
Advertise dainties through the dirt;
Have seen your coach-wheels splash rebuke
On virtue; and have learned your look

When, wealth and health slipped past, you stare
Along the streets alone, and there,
Round the long park, across the bridge,
The cold lamps at the pavement's edge
Wind on together and apart,
A fiery serpent for your heart.

Let the thoughts pass, an empty cloud!
Suppose I were to think aloud,—
What if to her all this were said?
Why, as a volume seldom read
Being opened halfway shuts again,
So might the pages of her brain
Be parted at such words, and thence
Close back upon the dusty sense.
For is there hue or shape defin'd
In Jenny's desecrated mind,
Where all contagious currents meet,
A Lethe of the middle street?
Nay, it reflects not any face,
Nor sound is in its sluggish pace,
But as they coil those eddies clot,
And night and day remember not.

Why, Jenny, you're asleep at last!—
Asleep, poor Jenny, hard and fast,—
So young and soft and tired; so fair,
With chin thus nestled in your hair,
Mouth quiet, eyelids almost blue
As if some sky of dreams shone through!

Just as another woman sleeps!
Enough to throw one's thoughts in heaps
Of doubt and horror,—what to say

Or think,—this awful secret sway,
The potter's power over the clay!
Of the same lump (it has been said)
For honour and dishonour made,
Two sister vessels. Here is one.

My cousin Nell is fond of fun,
And fond of dress, and change, and praise,
So mere a woman in her ways:
And if her sweet eyes rich in youth
Are like her lips that tell the truth,
My cousin Nell is fond of love.
And she's the girl I'm proudest of.
Who does not prize her, guard her well?
The love of change, in cousin Nell,
Shall find the best and hold it dear:
The unconquered mirth turn quieter
Not through her own, through others' woe:
The conscious pride of beauty glow
Beside another's pride in her,
One little part of all they share.
For Love himself shall ripen these
In a kind soil to just increase
Through years of fertilizing peace.

Of the same lump (as it is said)
For honour and dishonour made,
Two sister vessels. Here is one.

It makes a goblin of the sun.

So pure,—so fall'n! How dare to think
Of the first common kindred link?
Yet, Jenny, till the world shall burn

It seems that all things take their turn;
And who shall say but this fair tree
May need, in changes that may be,
Your children's children's charity?
Scorned then, no doubt, as you are scorn'd!
Shall no man hold his pride forewarn'd
Till in the end, the Day of Days,
At Judgment, one of his own race,
As frail and lost as you, shall rise,—
His daughter, with his mother's eyes?

How Jenny's clock ticks on the shelf!
Might not the dial scorn itself
That has such hours to register?
Yet as to me, even so to her
Are golden sun and silver moon,
In daily largesse of earth's boon,
Counted for life-coins to one tune.
And if, as blindfold fates are toss'd,
Through some one man this life be lost,
Shall soul not somehow pay for soul?

Fair shines the gilded aureole
In which our highest painters place
Some living woman's simple face.
And the stilled features thus descried
As Jenny's long throat droops aside,—
The shadows where the cheeks are thin,
And pure wide curve from ear to chin,—
With Raffael's, Leonardo's hand
To show them to men's souls, might stand,
Whole ages long, the whole world through,
For preachings of what God can do.
What has man done here? How atone,

Great God, for this which man has done?
And for the body and soul which by
Man's pitiless doom must now comply
With lifelong hell, what lullaby
Of sweet forgetful second birth
Remains? All dark. No sign on earth
What measure of God's rest endows
The many mansions of his house.

    If but a woman's heart might see
Such erring heart unerringly
For once! But that can never be.

    Like a rose shut in a book
In which pure women may not look,
For its base pages claim control
To crush the flower within the soul;
Where through each dead rose-leaf that clings,
Pale as transparent Psyche-wings,
To the vile text, are traced such things
As might make lady's cheek indeed
More than a living rose to read;
So nought save foolish foulness may
Watch with hard eyes the sure decay;
And so the life-blood of this rose,
Puddled with shameful knowledge, flows
Through leaves no chaste hand may unclose:
Yet still it keeps such faded show
Of when 'twas gathered long ago,
That the crushed petals' lovely grain,
The sweetness of the sanguine stain,
Seen of a woman's eyes, must make
Her pitiful heart, so prone to ache,
Love roses better for its sake:—

Only that this can never be:—
Even so unto her sex is she.

   Yet, Jenny, looking long at you,
The woman almost fades from view.
A cipher of man's changeless sum
Of lust, past, present, and to come,
Is left. A riddle that one shrinks
To challenge from the scornful sphinx.

   Like a toad within a stone
Seated while Time crumbles on;
Which sits there since the earth was curs'd
For Man's transgression at the first;
Which, living through all centuries,
Not once has seen the sun arise;
Whose life, to its cold circle charmed,
The earth's whole summers have not warmed;
Which always—whitherso the stone
Be flung—sits there, deaf, blind, alone;—
Aye, and shall not be driven out
Till that which shuts him round about
Break at the very Master's stroke,
And the dust thereof vanish as smoke,
And the seed of Man vanish as dust:—
Even so within this world is Lust.

   Come, come, what use in thoughts like this?
Poor little Jenny, good to kiss,—
You'd not believe by what strange roads
Thought travels, when your beauty goads
A man to-night to think of toads!
Jenny, wake up. . . . Why, there's the dawn!

And there's an early waggon drawn
To market, and some sheep that jog
Bleating before a barking dog;
And the old streets come peering through
Another night that London knew;
And all as ghostlike as the lamps.

So on the wings of day decamps
My last night's frolic. Glooms begin
To shiver off as lights creep in
Past the gauze curtains half drawn-to,
And the lamp's doubled shade grows blue,—
Your lamp, my Jenny, kept alight,
Like a wise virgin's, all one night!
And in the alcove coolly spread
Glimmers with dawn your empty bed;
And yonder your fair face I see
Reflected lying on my knee,
Where teems with first foreshadowings
Your pier-glass scrawled with diamond rings:
And on your bosom all night worn
Yesterday's rose now droops forlorn,
But dies not yet this summer morn.

And now without, as if some word
Had called upon them that they heard,
The London sparrows far and nigh
Clamour together suddenly;
And Jenny's cage-bird grown awake
Here in their song his part must take,
Because here too the day doth break.

And somehow in myself the dawn
Among stirred clouds and veils withdrawn

Strikes greyly on her. Let her sleep.
But will it wake her if I heap
These cushions thus beneath her head
Where my knee was? No,—there's your bed,
My Jenny, while you dream. And there
I lay among your golden hair,
Perhaps the subject of your dreams,
These golden coins.

               For still one deems
That Jenny's flattering sleep confers
New magic on the magic purse,—
Grim web, how clogged with shrivelled flies!
Between the threads fine fumes arise
And shape their pictures in the brain.
There roll no streets in glare and rain,
Nor flagrant man-swine whets his tusk;
But delicately sighs in musk
The homage of the dim boudoir;
Or like a palpitating star
Thrilled into song, the opera-night
Breathes faint in the quick pulse of light;
Or at the carriage-window shine
Rich wares for choice; or, free to dine,
Whirls through its hour of health (divine
For her) the concourse of the Park.
And though in the discounted dark
Her functions there and here are one,
Beneath the lamps and in the sun
There reigns at least the acknowledged belle
Apparelled beyond parallel.
Ah Jenny, yes, we know your dreams.

   For even the Paphian Venus seems
A goddess o'er the realms of love,

When silver-shrined in shadowy grove:
Aye, or let offerings nicely plac'd
But hide Priapus to the waist,
And whoso looks on him shall see
An eligible deity.

Why, Jenny, waking here alone
May help you to remember one,
Though all the memory's long outworn
Of many a double-pillowed morn.
I think I see you when you wake,
And rub your eyes for me, and shake
My gold, in rising, from your hair,
A Danaë for a moment there.

Jenny, my love rang true! for still
Love at first sight is vague, until
That tinkling makes him audible.

And must I mock you to the last,
Ashamed of my own shame,—aghast
Because some thoughts not born amiss
Rose at a poor fair face like this?
Well, of such thoughts so much I know:
In my life, as in hers, they show,
By a far gleam which I may near,
A dark path I can strive to clear.

Only one kiss. Good-bye, my dear.

Love's Nocturn

Master of the murmuring courts
    Where the shapes of sleep convene!—
Lo! my spirit here exhorts
    All the powers of thy demesne
    For their aid to woo my queen.
          What reports
    Yield thy jealous courts unseen?

Vaporous, unaccountable,
    Dreamworld lies forlorn of light,
Hollow like a breathing shell.
    Ah! that from all dreams I might
    Choose one dream and guide its flight!
          I know well
    What her sleep should tell to-night.

There the dreams are multitudes:
    Some that will not wait for sleep,
Deep within the August woods;
    Some that hum while rest may steep
    Weary labour laid a-heap;
          Interludes,
    Some, of grievous moods that weep.

Poets' fancies all are there:
    There the elf-girls flood with wings
Valleys full of plaintive air;
    There breathe perfumes; there in rings
    Whirl the foam-bewildered springs;
          Siren there
    Winds her dizzy hair and sings.

Thence the one dream mutually
    Dreamed in bridal unison,
Less than waking ecstasy;
    Half-formed visions that make moan
    In the house of birth alone;
            And what we
    At death's wicket see, unknown.

But for mine own sleep, it lies
    In one gracious form's control,
Fair with honourable eyes,
    Lamps of a translucent soul:
    O their glance is loftiest dole,
            Sweet and wise,
    Wherein Love descries his goal.

Reft of her, my dreams are all
    Clammy trance that fears the sky:
Changing footpaths shift and fall;
    From polluted coverts nigh,
    Miserable phantoms sigh;
            Quakes the pall,
    And the funeral goes by.

Master, is it soothly said
    That, as echoes of man's speech
Far in secret clefts are made,
    So do all men's bodies reach
    Shadows o'er thy sunken beach,—
            Shape or shade
    In those halls pourtrayed of each?

Ah! might I, by thy good grace
    Groping in the windy stair,

(Darkness and the breath of space
  Like loud waters everywhere,)
    Meeting mine own image there
        Face to face,
Send it from that place to her!

Nay, not I; but oh! do thou,
  Master, from thy shadowkind
Call my body's phantom now:
    Bid it bear its face declin'd
    Till its flight her slumbers find,
        And her brow
  Feel its presence bow like wind.

Where in groves the gracile Spring
  Trembles, with mute orison
Confidently strengthening,
    Water's voice and wind's as one
    Shed an echo in the sun.
        Soft as Spring,
  Master, bid it sing and moan.

Song shall tell how glad and strong
  Is the night she soothes alway;
Moan shall grieve with that parched tongue
  Of the brazen hours of day:
    Sounds as of the springtide they,
        Moan and song,
  While the chill months long for May.

Not the prayers which with all leave
  The world's fluent woes prefer,—
Not the praise the world doth give,
  Dulcet fulsome whisperer;—

Let it yield my love to her,
            And achieve
Strength that shall not grieve or err.

Wheresoe'er my dreams befall,
    Both at night-watch, (let it say,)
And where round the sundial
    The reluctant hours of day,
    Heartless, hopeless of their way,
            Rest and call;—
    There her glance doth fall and stay.

Suddenly her face is there:
    So do mounting vapours wreathe
Subtle-scented transports where
    The black firwood sets its teeth.
    Part the boughs and look beneath,—
            Lilies share
    Secret waters there, and breathe.

Master, bid my shadow bend
    Whispering thus till birth of light,
Lest new shapes that sleep may send
    Scatter all its work to flight;—
    Master, master of the night,
            Bid it spend
    Speech, song, prayer, and end aright.

Yet, ah me! if at her head
    There another phantom lean
Murmuring o'er the fragrant bed,—
    Ah! and if my spirit's queen
    Smile those alien prayers between,—

Ah! poor shade!
Shall it strive, or fade unseen?

How should love's own messenger
　　Strive with love and be love's foe?
Master, nay! If thus, in her,
　　Sleep a wedded heart should show,—
　　Silent let mine image go,
　　　　Its old share
Of thy spell-bound air to know.

Like a vapour wan and mute,
　　Like a flame, so let it pass;
One low sigh across her lute,
　　One dull breath against her glass;
　　And to my sad soul, alas!
　　　　One salute
Cold as when Death's foot shall pass.

Then, too, let all hopes of mine,
　　All vain hopes by night and day,
Slowly at thy summoning sign
　　Rise up pallid and obey.
　　Dreams, if this is thus, were they:—
　　　　Be they thine,
And to dreamworld pine away.

Yet from old time, life, not death,
　　Master, in thy rule is rife:
Lo! through thee, with mingling breath,
　　Adam woke beside his wife.
　　O Love, bring me so, for strife,
　　　　Force and faith,
Bring me so not death but life!

Yea, to Love himself is pour'd
    This frail song of hope and fear.
Thou art Love, of one accord
    With kind Sleep to bring her near,
    Still-eyed, deep-eyed, ah how dear!
            Master, Lord,
    In her name implor'd, O hear!

The House of Life: A Sonnet-Sequence

A Sonnet is a moment's monument,—
  Memorial from the Soul's eternity
  To one dead deathless hour. Look that it be,
Whether for lustral rite or dire portent,
Of its own arduous fulness reverent:
  Carve it in ivory or in ebony,
  As Day or Night may rule; and let Time see
Its flowering crest impearled and orient.

A Sonnet is a coin: its face reveals
  The soul,—its converse, to what Power 'tis due:—
Whether for tribute to the august appeals
  Of Life, or dower in Love's high retinue,
It serve; or, 'mid the dark wharf's cavernous breath,
In Charon's palm it pay the toll to Death.

Part I. *Youth and Change*

♦ ♦ ♦ ♦

SONNET I   LOVE ENTHRONED

I marked all kindred Powers the heart finds fair:—
    Truth, with awed lips; and Hope, with eyes upcast;
    And Fame, whose loud wings fan the ashen Past
To signal-fires, Oblivion's flight to scare;
And Youth, with still some single golden hair
    Unto his shoulder clinging, since the last
    Embrace wherein two sweet arms held him fast;
And Life, still wreathing flowers for Death to wear.

Love's throne was not with these; but far above
    All passionate wind of welcome and farewell
He sat in breathless bowers they dream not of;
    Though Truth foreknow Love's heart, and Hope foretell,
    And Fame be for Love's sake desirable,
And Youth be dear, and Life be sweet to Love.

SONNET II   BRIDAL BIRTH

As when desire, long darkling, dawns, and first
    The mother looks upon the newborn child,
    Even so my Lady stood at gaze and smiled
When her soul knew at length the Love it nurs'd.
Born with her life, creature of poignant thirst
    And exquisite hunger, at her heart Love lay
    Quickening in darkness, till a voice that day
Cried on him, and the bonds of birth were burst.

Now, shadowed by his wings, our faces yearn
    Together, as his full-grown feet now range
        The grove, and his warm hands our couch prepare:
Till to his song our bodiless souls in turn
    Be born his children, when Death's nuptial change
        Leaves us for light the halo of his hair.

SONNET III   LOVE'S TESTAMENT

O thou who at Love's hour ecstatically
   Unto my heart dost evermore present,
   Clothed with his fire, thy heart his testament;
Whom I have neared and felt thy breath to be
The inmost incense of his sanctuary;
   Who without speech hast owned him, and, intent
   Upon his will, thy life with mine hast blent,
And murmured, "I am thine, thou'rt one with me!"

O what from thee the grace, to me the prize,
   And what to Love the glory,—when the whole
   Of the deep stair thou tread'st to the dim shoal
And weary water of the place of sighs,
And there dost work deliverance, as thine eyes
   Draw up my prisoned spirit to thy soul!

SONNET IV   LOVESIGHT

When do I see thee most, beloved one?
   When in the light the spirits of mine eyes
   Before thy face, their altar, solemnize
The worship of that Love through thee made known?
Or when in the dusk hours, (we two alone,)
   Close-kissed and eloquent of still replies
   Thy twilight-hidden glimmering visage lies,
And my soul only sees thy soul its own?

O love, my love! if I no more should see
Thyself, nor on the earth the shadow of thee,
   Nor image of thine eyes in any spring,—
How then should sound upon Life's darkening slope
The ground-whirl of the perished leaves of Hope,
   The wind of Death's imperishable wing?

SONNET V HEART'S HOPE

By what word's power, the key of paths untrod,
    Shall I the difficult deeps of Love explore,
    Till parted waves of Song yield up the shore
Even as that sea which Israel crossed dryshod?
For lo! in some poor rhythmic period,
    Lady, I fain would tell how evermore
    Thy soul I know not from thy body, nor
Thee from myself, neither our love from God.

Yea, in God's name, and Love's, and thine, would I
    Draw from one loving heart such evidence
As to all hearts all things shall signify;
    Tender as dawn's first hill-fire, and intense
    As instantaneous penetrating sense,
In Spring's birth-hour, of other Springs gone by.

SONNET VI THE KISS

What smouldering senses in death's sick delay
    Or seizure of malign vicissitude
    Can rob this body of honour, or denude
This soul of wedding-raiment worn to-day?
For lo! even now my lady's lips did play
    With these my lips such consonant interlude
    As laurelled Orpheus longed for when he wooed
The half-drawn hungering face with that last lay.

I was a child beneath her touch,—a man
    When breast to breast we clung, even I and she,—
    A spirit when her spirit looked through me,—
A god when all our life-breath met to fan
Our life-blood, till love's emulous ardours ran,
    Fire within fire, desire in deity.

SONNET VIa   NUPTIAL SLEEP

At length their long kiss severed, with sweet smart:
    And as the last slow sudden drops are shed
    From sparkling eaves when all the storm has fled,
So singly flagged the pulses of each heart.
Their bosoms sundered, with the opening start
    Of married flowers to either side outspread
    From the knit stem; yet still their mouths, burnt red,
Fawned on each other where they lay apart.

Sleep sank them lower than the tide of dreams,
    And their dreams watched them sink, and slid away.
Slowly their souls swam up again, through gleams
    Of watered light and dull drowned waifs of day;
Till from some wonder of new woods and streams
    He woke, and wondered more: for there she lay.

SONNET VII   SUPREME SURRENDER

To all the spirits of Love that wander by
    Along his love-sown harvest-field of sleep
    My lady lies apparent; and the deep
Calls to the deep; and no man sees but I.
The bliss so long afar, at length so nigh,
    Rests there attained. Methinks proud Love must weep
    When Fate's control doth from his harvest reap
The sacred hour for which the years did sigh.

First touched, the hand now warm around my neck
    Taught memory long to mock desire: and lo!
    Across my breast the abandoned hair doth flow,
Where one shorn tress long stirred the longing ache:
And next the heart that trembled for its sake
    Lies the queen-heart in sovereign overthrow.

Some ladies love the jewels in Love's zone,
 And gold-tipped darts he hath for painless play
 In idle scornful hours he flings away;
And some that listen to his lute's soft tone
Do love to vaunt the silver praise their own;
 Some prize his blindfold sight; and there be they
 Who kissed his wings which brought him yesterday
And thank his wings to-day that he is flown.

My lady only loves the heart of Love:
 Therefore Love's heart, my lady, hath for thee
 His bower of unimagined flower and tree:
There kneels he now, and all-anhungered of
Thine eyes grey-lit in shadowing hair above,
 Seals with thy mouth his immortality.

SONNET IX   PASSION AND WORSHIP

One flame-winged brought a white-winged harp-player
 Even where my lady and I lay all alone;
 Saying: "Behold, this minstrel is unknown;
Bid him depart, for I am minstrel here:
Only my strains are to Love's dear ones dear."
 Then said I: "Through thine hautboy's rapturous tone
 Unto my lady still this harp makes moan,
And still she deems the cadence deep and clear."

Then said my lady: "Thou art Passion of Love,
 And this Love's Worship: both he plights to me.
 Thy mastering music walks the sunlit sea:
But where wan water trembles in the grove
And the wan moon is all the light thereof,
 This harp still makes my name its voluntary."

SONNET X   THE PORTRAIT

O Lord of all compassionate control,
　　O Love! let this my lady's picture glow
　　Under my hand to praise her name, and show
Even of her inner self the perfect whole:
That he who seeks her beauty's furthest goal,
　　Beyond the light that the sweet glances throw
　　And refluent wave of the sweet smile, may know
The very sky and sea-line of her soul.

Lo! it is done. Above the enthroning throat
　　The mouth's mould testifies of voice and kiss,
　　　The shadowed eyes remember and foresee.
Her face is made her shrine. Let all men note
　　That in all years (O Love, thy gift is this!)
　　　They that would look on her must come to me.

SONNET XI   THE LOVE-LETTER

Warmed by her hand and shadowed by her hair
　　As close she leaned and poured her heart through thee,
　　Whereof the articulate throbs accompany
The smooth black stream that makes thy whiteness fair,—
Sweet fluttering sheet, even of her breath aware,—
　　Oh let thy silent song disclose to me
　　That soul wherewith her lips and eyes agree
Like married music in Love's answering air.

Fain had I watched her when, at some fond thought,
　　Her bosom to the writing closelier press'd,
　　And her breast's secrets peered into her breast;
When, through eyes raised an instant, her soul sought
My soul, and from the sudden confluence caught
　　The words that made her love the loveliest.

SONNET XII   THE LOVERS' WALK

Sweet twining hedgeflowers wind-stirred in no wise
   On this June day; and hand that clings in hand:—
     Still glades; and meeting faces scarcely fann'd:—
An osier-odoured stream that draws the skies
Deep to its heart; and mirrored eyes in eyes:—
   Fresh hourly wonder o'er the Summer land
     Of light and cloud; and two souls softly spann'd
With one o'erarching heaven of smiles and sighs:—

Even such their path, whose bodies lean unto
   Each other's visible sweetness amorously,—
     Whose passionate hearts lean by Love's high decree
Together on his heart for ever true,
As the cloud-foaming firmamental blue
   Rests on the blue line of a foamless sea.

SONNET XIII   YOUTH'S ANTIPHONY

"I love you, sweet: how can you ever learn
   How much I love you?" "You I love even so,
     And so I learn it." "Sweet, you cannot know
How fair you are." "If fair enough to earn
Your love, so much is all my love's concern."
   "My love grows hourly, sweet." "Mine too doth grow,
     Yet love seemed full so many hours ago!"
Thus lovers speak, till kisses claim their turn.

Ah! happy they to whom such words as these
   In youth have served for speech the whole day long,
     Hour after hour, remote from the world's throng,
Work, contest, fame, all life's confederate pleas,—
   What while Love breathed in sighs and silences
     Through two blent souls one rapturous undersong.

SONNET XIV   YOUTH'S SPRING-TRIBUTE

On this sweet bank your head thrice sweet and dear
    I lay, and spread your hair on either side,
    And see the newborn woodflowers bashful-eyed
Look through the golden tresses here and there.
On these debateable borders of the year
    Spring's foot half falters; scarce she yet may know
    The leafless blackthorn-blossom from the snow;
And through her bowers the wind's way still is clear.

But April's sun strikes down the glades to-day;
    So shut your eyes upturned, and feel my kiss
Creep, as the Spring now thrills through every spray,
    Up your warm throat to your warm lips: for this
    Is even the hour of Love's sworn suitservice,
With whom cold hearts are counted castaway.

SONNET XV   THE BIRTH-BOND

Have you not noted, in some family
    Where two were born of a first marriage-bed,
    How still they own their gracious bond, though fed
And nursed on the forgotten breast and knee?—
How to their father's children they shall be
    In act and thought of one goodwill; but each
    Shall for the other have, in silence speech,
And in a word complete community?

Even so, when first I saw you, seemed it, love,
    That among souls allied to mine was yet
One nearer kindred than life hinted of.
    O born with me somewhere that men forget,
    And though in years of sight and sound unmet,
Known for my soul's birth-partner well enough!

SONNET XVI   A DAY OF LOVE

Those envied places which do know her well,
   And are so scornful of this lonely place,
   Even now for once are emptied of her grace:
Nowhere but here she is: and while Love's spell
From his predominant presence doth compel
   All alien hours, an outworn populace,
   The hours of Love fill full the echoing space
With sweet confederate music favourable.

Now many memories make solicitous
   The delicate love-lines of her mouth, till, lit
   With quivering fire, the words take wing from it;
As here between our kisses we sit thus
   Speaking of things remembered, and so sit
Speechless while things forgotten call to us.

SONNET XVII   BEAUTY'S PAGEANT

What dawn-pulse at the heart of heaven, or last
   Incarnate flower of culminating day,—
   What marshalled marvels on the skirts of May,
Or song full-quired, sweet June's encomiast;
What glory of change by Nature's hand amass'd
   Can vie with all those moods of varying grace
   Which o'er one loveliest woman's form and face
Within this hour, within this room, have pass'd?

Love's very vesture and elect disguise
   Was each fine movement,—wonder new-begot
   Of lily or swan or swan-stemmed galiot;
Joy to his sight who now the sadlier sighs,
   Parted again; and sorrow yet for eyes
   Unborn, that read these words and saw her not.

Beauty like hers is genius. Not the call
   Of Homer's or of Dante's heart sublime,—
   Not Michael's hand furrowing the zones of time,—
Is more with compassed mysteries musical;
Nay, not in Spring's or Summer's sweet footfall
   More gathered gifts exuberant Life bequeaths
   Than doth this sovereign face, whose love-spell breathes
Even from its shadowed contour on the wall.

As many men are poets in their youth,
   But for one sweet-strung soul the wires prolong
   Even through all change the indomitable song;
So in like wise the envenomed years, whose tooth
Rends shallower grace with ruin void of ruth,
   Upon this beauty's power shall wreak no wrong.

SONNET XIX   SILENT NOON

Your hands lie open in the long fresh grass,—
   The finger-points look through like rosy blooms:
   Your eyes smile peace. The pasture gleams and glooms
'Neath billowing skies that scatter and amass.
All round our nest, far as the eye can pass,
   Are golden kingcup-fields with silver edge
   Where the cow-parsley skirts the hawthorn-hedge.
'Tis visible silence, still as the hour-glass.

Deep in the sun-searched growths the dragon-fly
Hangs like a blue thread loosened from the sky:—
   So this wing'd hour is dropt to us from above.
Oh! clasp we to our hearts, for deathless dower,
This close-companioned inarticulate hour
   When twofold silence was the song of love.

SONNET XX   GRACIOUS MOONLIGHT

Even as the moon grows queenlier in mid-space
    When the sky darkens, and her cloud-rapt car
    Thrills with intenser radiance from afar,—
So lambent, lady, beams thy sovereign grace
When the drear soul desires thee. Of that face
    What shall be said,—which, like a governing star,
    Gathers and garners from all things that are
Their silent penetrative loveliness?

O'er water-daisies and wild waifs of Spring,
    There where the iris rears its gold-crowned sheaf
    With flowering rush and sceptred arrow-leaf,
So have I marked Queen Dian, in bright ring
Of cloud above and wave below, take wing
    And chase night's gloom, as thou the spirit's grief.

SONNET XXI   LOVE-SWEETNESS

Sweet dimness of her loosened hair's downfall
    About thy face; her sweet hands round thy head
    In gracious fostering union garlanded;
Her tremulous smiles; her glances' sweet recall
Of love; her murmuring sighs memorial;
    Her mouth's culled sweetness by thy kisses shed
    On cheeks and neck and eyelids, and so led
Back to her mouth which answers there for all:—

What sweeter than these things, except the thing
    In lacking which all these would lose their sweet:—
    The confident heart's still fervour: the swift beat
And soft subsidence of the spirit's wing,
Then when it feels, in cloud-girt wayfaring,
    The breath of kindred plumes against its feet?

SONNET XXII   HEART'S HAVEN

Sometimes she is a child within mine arms,
  Cowering beneath dark wings that love must chase,—
  With still tears showering and averted face,
Inexplicably filled with faint alarms:
And oft from mine own spirit's hurtling harms
  I crave the refuge of her deep embrace,—
  Against all ills the fortified strong place
And sweet reserve of sovereign counter-charms.

And Love, our light at night and shade at noon,
  Lulls us to rest with songs, and turns away
  All shafts of shelterless tumultuous day.
Like the moon's growth, his face gleams through his tune;
And as soft waters warble to the moon,
  Our answering spirits chime one roundelay.

SONNET XXIII   LOVE'S BAUBLES

I stood where Love in brimming armfuls bore
  Slight wanton flowers and foolish toys of fruit:
  And round him ladies thronged in warm pursuit,
Fingered and lipped and proffered the strange store.
And from one hand the petal and the core
  Savoured of sleep; and cluster and curled shoot
  Seemed from another hand like shame's salute,—
Gifts that I felt my cheek was blushing for.

At last Love bade my Lady give the same:
  And as I looked, the dew was light thereon;
  And as I took them, at her touch they shone
With inmost heaven-hue of the heart of flame.
And then Love said: "Lo! when the hand is hers,
Follies of love are love's true ministers."

SONNET XXIV PRIDE OF YOUTH

Even as a child, of sorrow that we give
   The dead, but little in his heart can find,
   Since without need of thought to his clear mind
Their turn it is to die and his to live:—
Even so the winged New Love smiles to receive
   Along his eddying plumes the auroral wind,
   Nor, forward glorying, casts one look behind
Where night-rack shrouds the Old Love fugitive.

There is a change in every hour's recall,
   And the last cowslip in the fields we see
   On the same day with the first corn-poppy.
Alas for hourly change! Alas for all
The loves that from his hand proud Youth lets fall,
   Even as the beads of a told rosary!

SONNET XXV WINGED HOURS

Each hour until we meet is as a bird
   That wings from far his gradual way along
   The rustling covert of my soul,—his song
Still loudlier trilled through leaves more deeply stirr'd:
But at the hour of meeting, a clear word
   Is every note he sings, in Love's own tongue;
   Yet, Love, thou know'st the sweet strain suffers wrong
Full oft through our contending joys unheard.

What of that hour at last, when for her sake
   No wing may fly to me nor song may flow;
   When, wandering round my life unleaved, I know
The bloodied feathers scattered in the brake,
And think how she, far from me, with like eyes
Sees through the untuneful bough the wingless skies?

SONNET XXVI   MID-RAPTURE

Thou lovely and beloved, thou my love;
   Whose kiss seems still the first; whose summoning eyes,
   Even now, as for our love-world's new sunrise,
Shed very dawn; whose voice, attuned above
All modulation of the deep-bowered dove,
   Is like a hand laid softly on the soul;
   Whose hand is like a sweet voice to control
Those worn tired brows it hath the keeping of:—

What word can answer to thy word,—what gaze
   To thine, which now absorbs within its sphere
   My worshipping face, till I am mirrored there
Light-circled in a heaven of deep-drawn rays?
What clasp, what kiss mine inmost heart can prove,
O lovely and beloved, O my love?

SONNET XXVII   HEART'S COMPASS

Sometimes thou seem'st not as thyself alone,
   But as the meaning of all things that are;
   A breathless wonder, shadowing forth afar
Some heavenly solstice hushed and halcyon;
Whose unstirred lips are music's visible tone;
   Whose eyes the sun-gate of the soul unbar,
   Being of its furthest fires oracular;—
The evident heart of all life sown and mown.

Even such Love is; and is not thy name Love?
   Yea, by thy hand the Love-god rends apart
   All gathering clouds of Night's ambiguous art;
Flings them far down, and sets thine eyes above;
And simply, as some gage of flower or glove,
   Stakes with a smile the world against thy heart.

SONNET XXVIII   SOUL-LIGHT

What other woman could be loved like you,
   Or how of you should love possess his fill?
   After the fulness of all rapture, still,—
As at the end of some deep avenue
A tender glamour of day,—there comes to view
   Far in your eyes a yet more hungering thrill,—
   Such fire as Love's soul-winnowing hands distil
Even from his inmost ark of light and dew.

And as the traveller triumphs with the sun,
   Glorying in heat's mid-height, yet startide brings
   Wonder new-born, and still fresh transport springs
From limpid lambent hours of day begun;—
Even so, through eyes and voice, your soul doth move
My soul with changeful light of infinite love.

SONNET XXIX   THE MOONSTAR

Lady, I thank thee for thy loveliness,
   Because my lady is more lovely still.
   Glorying I gaze, and yield with glad goodwill
To thee thy tribute; by whose sweet-spun dress
Of delicate life Love labours to assess
   My lady's absolute queendom; saying, "Lo!
   How high this beauty is, which yet doth show
But as that beauty's sovereign votaress."

Lady, I saw thee with her, side by side;
   And as, when night's fair fires their queen surround,
An emulous star too near the moon will ride,—
   Even so thy rays within her luminous bound
   Were traced no more; and by the light so drown'd,
Lady, not thou but she was glorified.

Love, through your spirit and mine what summer eve
   Now glows with glory of all things possess'd,
   Since this day's sun of rapture filled the west
And the light sweetened as the fire took leave?
Awhile now softlier let your bosom heave,
   As in Love's harbour, even that loving breast,
   All care takes refuge while we sink to rest,
And mutual dreams the bygone bliss retrieve.

Many the days that Winter keeps in store,
   Sunless throughout, or whose brief sun-glimpses
   Scarce shed the heaped snow through the naked trees,
This day at least was Summer's paramour,
Sun-coloured to the imperishable core
   With sweet well-being of love and full heart's ease.

SONNET XXXI   HER GIFTS

High grace, the dower of queens; and therewithal
   Some wood-born wonder's sweet simplicity;
   A glance like water brimming with the sky
Or hyacinth-light where forest-shadows fall;
Such thrilling pallor of cheek as doth enthral
   The heart; a mouth whose passionate forms imply
   All music and all silence held thereby;
Deep golden locks, her sovereign coronal;
A round reared neck, meet column of Love's shrine
   To cling to when the heart takes sanctuary;
   Hands which for ever at Love's bidding be,
And soft-stirred feet still answering to his sign:—
These are her gifts, as tongue may tell them o'er.
Breathe low her name, my soul; for that means more.

Not by one measure mayst thou mete our love;
　　For how should I be loved as I love thee?—
　　I, graceless, joyless, lacking absolutely
All gifts that with thy queenship best behove;—
Thou, throned in every heart's elect alcove,
　　And crowned with garlands culled from every tree,
　　Which for no head but thine, by Love's decree,
All beauties and all mysteries interwove.

But here thine eyes and lips yield soft rebuke:—
　　"Then only" (say'st thou) "could I love thee less,
　　　When thou couldst doubt my love's equality."
Peace, sweet! If not to sum but worth we look,—
　　Thy heart's transcendence, not my heart's excess,—
　　　Then more a thousandfold thou lov'st than I.

Could Juno's self more sovereign presence wear
　　Than thou, 'mid other ladies throned in grace?—
　　Or Pallas, when thou bend'st with soul-stilled face
O'er poet's page gold-shadowed in thy hair?
Dost thou than Venus seem less heavenly fair
　　When o'er the sea of love's tumultuous trance
　　Hovers thy smile, and mingles with thy glance
That sweet voice like the last wave murmuring there?

Before such triune loveliness divine
　　Awestruck I ask, which goddess here most claims
The prize that, howsoe'er adjudged, is thine?
　　Then Love breathes low the sweetest of thy names;
And Venus Victrix to my heart doth bring
Herself, the Helen of her guerdoning.

SONNET XXXIV   THE DARK GLASS

Not I myself know all my love for thee:
  How should I reach so far, who cannot weigh
  To-morrow's dower by gage of yesterday?
Shall birth and death, and all dark names that be
As doors and windows bared to some loud sea,
  Lash deaf mine ears and blind my face with spray;
  And shall my sense pierce love,—the last relay
And ultimate outpost of eternity?

Lo! what am I to Love, the lord of all?
  One murmuring shell he gathers from the sand,—
  One little heart-flame sheltered in his hand.
Yet through thine eyes he grants me clearest call
And veriest touch of powers primordial
  That any hour-girt life may understand.

SONNET XXXV   THE LAMP'S SHRINE

Sometimes I fain would find in thee some fault,
  That I might love thee still in spite of it:
  Yet how should our Lord Love curtail one whit
Thy perfect praise whom most he would exalt?
Alas! he can but make my heart's low vault
  Even in men's sight unworthier, being lit
  By thee, who thereby show'st more exquisite
Like fiery chrysoprase in deep basalt.

Yet will I nowise shrink; but at Love's shrine
  Myself within the beams his brow doth dart
  Will set the flashing jewel of thy heart
In that dull chamber where it deigns to shine:
For lo! in honour of thine excellencies
My heart takes pride to show how poor it is.

SONNET XXXVI   LIFE-IN-LOVE

Not in thy body is thy life at all,
    But in this lady's lips and hands and eyes;
    Through these she yields thee life that vivifies
What else were sorrow's servant and death's thrall.
Look on thyself without her, and recall
    The waste remembrance and forlorn surmise
    That lived but in a dead-drawn breath of sighs
O'er vanished hours and hours eventual.

Even so much life hath the poor tress of hair
    Which, stored apart, is all love hath to show
    For heart-beats and for fire-heats long ago;
Even so much life endures unknown, even where,
'Mid change the changeless night environeth,
Lies all that golden hair undimmed in death.

SONNET XL   SEVERED SELVES

Two separate divided silences,
    Which, brought together, would find loving voice;
    Two glances which together would rejoice
In love, now lost like stars beyond dark trees;
Two hands apart whose touch alone gives ease;
    Two bosoms which, heart-shrined with mutual flame,
    Would, meeting in one clasp, be made the same;
Two souls, the shores wave-mocked of sundering seas:—

Such are we now. Ah! may our hope forecast
    Indeed one hour again, when on this stream
    Of darkened love once more the light shall gleam?—
An hour how slow to come, how quickly past,—
Which blooms and fades, and only leaves at last,
    Faint as shed flowers, the attenuated dream.

SONNET XLI   THROUGH DEATH TO LOVE

Like labour-laden moonclouds faint to flee
   From winds that sweep the winter-bitten wold,—
   Like multiform circumfluence manifold
Of night's flood-tide,—like terrors that agree
Of hoarse-tongued fire and inarticulate sea,—
   Even such, within some glass dimmed by our breath,
   Our hearts discern wild images of Death,
Shadows and shoals that edge eternity.

Howbeit athwart Death's imminent shade doth soar
   One Power, than flow of stream or flight of dove
   Sweeter to glide around, to brood above.
Tell me, my heart,—what angel-greeted door
Or threshold of wing-winnowed threshing-floor
   Hath guest fire-fledged as thine, whose lord is Love?

SONNET XLII   HOPE OVERTAKEN

I deemed thy garments, O my Hope, were grey,
   So far I viewed thee. Now the space between
   Is passed at length; and garmented in green
Even as in days of yore thou stand'st to-day.
Ah God! and but for lingering dull dismay,
   On all that road our footsteps erst had been
   Even thus commingled, and our shadows seen
Blent on the hedgerows and the water-way.

O Hope of mine whose eyes are living love,
   No eyes but hers,—O Love and Hope the same!—
   Lean close to me, for now the sinking sun
That warmed our feet scarce gilds our hair above.
   O hers thy voice and very hers thy name!
   Alas, cling round me, for the day is done!

SONNET XXXVII   THE LOVE-MOON

"When that dead face, bowered in the furthest years,
  Which once was all the life years held for thee,
  Can now scarce bid the tides of memory
Cast on thy soul a little spray of tears,—
How canst thou gaze into these eyes of hers
  Whom now thy heart delights in, and not see
  Within each orb Love's philtred euphrasy
Make them of buried troth remembrancers?"

"Nay, pitiful Love, nay, loving Pity! Well
  Thou knowest that in these twain I have confess'd
Two very voices of thy summoning bell.
  Nay, Master, shall not Death make manifest
In these the culminant changes which approve
The love-moon that must light my soul to Love?"

SONNET XXXVIII   THE MORROW'S MESSAGE

"Thou Ghost," I said, "and is thy name To-day?—
  Yesterday's son, with such an abject brow!—
  And can To-morrow be more pale than thou?"
While yet I spoke, the silence answered: "Yea,
Henceforth our issue is all grieved and grey,
  And each beforehand makes such poor avow
  As of old leaves beneath the budding bough
Or night-drift that the sundawn shreds away."

Then cried I: "Mother of many malisons,
  O Earth, receive me to thy dusty bed!"
  But therewithal the tremulous silence said:
"Lo! Love yet bids thy lady greet thee once:—
Yea, twice,—whereby thy life is still the sun's;
  And thrice,—whereby the shadow of death is dead."

SONNET XXXIX   SLEEPLESS DREAMS

Girt in dark growths, yet glimmering with one star,
  O night desirous as the nights of youth!
  Why should my heart within thy spell, forsooth,
Now beat, as the bride's finger-pulses are
Quickened within the girdling golden bar?
  What wings are these that fan my pillow smooth?
  And why does Sleep, waved back by Joy and Ruth,
Tread softly round and gaze at me from far?

Nay, night deep-leaved! And would Love feign in thee
  Some shadowy palpitating grove that bears
  Rest for man's eyes and music for his ears?
O lonely night! art thou not known to me,
A thicket hung with masks of mockery
  And watered with the wasteful warmth of tears?

SONNET XLIII   LOVE AND HOPE

Bless love and hope. Full many a withered year
  Whirled past us, eddying to its chill doomsday;
  And clasped together where the blown leaves lay
We long have knelt and wept full many a tear.
Yet lo! one hour at last, the Spring's compeer,
  Flutes softly to us from some green byeway:
  Those years, those tears are dead, but only they:—
Bless love and hope, true soul; for we are here.

Cling heart to heart; nor of this hour demand
  Whether in very truth, when we are dead,
  Our hearts shall wake to know Love's golden head
Sole sunshine of the imperishable land;
Or but discern, through night's unfeatured scope,
Scorn-fired at length the illusive eyes of Hope.

SONNET XLIV   CLOUD AND WIND

Love, should I fear death most for you or me?
   Yet if you die, can I not follow you,
   Forcing the straits of change? Alas! but who
Shall wrest a bond from night's inveteracy,
Ere yet my hazardous soul put forth, to be
   Her warrant against all her haste might rue?—
   Ah! in your eyes so reached what dumb adieu,
What unsunned gyres of waste eternity?

And if I die the first, shall death be then
   A lampless watchtower whence I see you weep?—
   Or (woe is me!) a bed wherein my sleep
Ne'er notes (as death's dear cup at last you drain),
The hour when you too learn that all is vain
   And that Hope sows what Love shall never reap?

SONNET XLV   SECRET PARTING

Because our talk was of the cloud-control
   And moon-track of the journeying face of Fate,
   Her tremulous kisses faltered at love's gate
And her eyes dreamed against a distant goal:
But soon, remembering her how brief the whole
   Of joy, which its own hours annihilate,
   Her set gaze gathered, thirstier than of late,
And as she kissed, her mouth became her soul.

Thence in what ways we wandered, and how strove
   To build with fire-tried vows the piteous home
   Which memory haunts and whither sleep may roam,—
They only know for whom the roof of Love
Is the still-seated secret of the grove,
   Nor spire may rise nor bell be heard therefrom.

SONNET XLVI   PARTED LOVE

What shall be said of this embattled day
  And armèd occupation of this night
   By all thy foes beleaguered,—now when sight
Nor sound denotes the loved one far away?
Of these thy vanquished hours what shalt thou say,—
  As every sense to which she dealt delight
   Now labours lonely o'er the stark noon-height
To reach the sunset's desolate disarray?

Stand still, fond fettered wretch! while Memory's art
  Parades the Past before thy face, and lures
   Thy spirit to her passionate portraitures:
Till the tempestuous tide-gates flung apart
Flood with wild will the hollows of thy heart,
  And thy heart rends thee, and thy body endures.

SONNET XLVII   BROKEN MUSIC

The mother will not turn, who thinks she hears
  Her nursling's speech first grow articulate;
   But breathless with averted eyes elate
She sits, with open lips and open ears,
That it may call her twice. 'Mid doubts and fears
  Thus oft my soul has hearkened; till the song,
   A central moan for days, at length found tongue,
And the sweet music welled and the sweet tears.

But now, whatever while the soul is fain
  To list that wonted murmur, as it were
The speech-bound sea-shell's low importunate strain,—
  No breath of song, thy voice alone is there,
O bitterly beloved! and all her gain
  Is but the pang of unpermitted prayer.

There came an image in Life's retinue
    That had Love's wings and bore his gonfalon:
    Fair was the web, and nobly wrought thereon,
O soul-sequestered face, thy form and hue!
Bewildering sounds, such as Spring wakens to,
    Shook in its folds; and through my heart its power
    Sped trackless as the immemorable hour
When birth's dark portal groaned and all was new.

But a veiled woman followed, and she caught
    The banner round its staff, to furl and cling,—
    Then plucked a feather from the bearer's wing
And held it to his lips that stirred it not,
And said to me, "Behold, there is no breath:
I and this Love are one, and I am Death."

SONNETS XLIX, L, LI, LII WILLOWWOOD

I

I sat with Love upon a woodside well,
    Leaning across the water, I and he;
    Nor ever did he speak nor looked at me,
But touched his lute wherein was audible
The certain secret thing he had to tell:
    Only our mirrored eyes met silently
    In the low wave; and that sound came to be
The passionate voice I knew; and my tears fell.

And at their fall, his eyes beneath grew hers;
And with his foot and with his wing-feathers
    He swept the spring that watered my heart's drouth.
Then the dark ripples spread to waving hair,
And as I stooped, her own lips rising there
    Bubbled with brimming kisses at my mouth.

II

And now Love sang: but his was such a song,
    So meshed with half-remembrance hard to free,
    As souls disused in death's sterility
May sing when the new birthday tarries long.
And I was made aware of a dumb throng
    That stood aloof, one form by every tree,
    All mournful forms, for each was I or she,
The shades of those our days that had no tongue.

They looked on us, and knew us and were known;
    While fast together, alive from the abyss,
    Clung the soul-wrung implacable close kiss;
And pity of self through all made broken moan
Which said "For once, for once, for once alone!"
    And still Love sang, and what he sang was this:—

"O ye, all ye that walk in Willowwood,
    That walk with hollow faces burning white;
What fathom-depth of soul-struck widowhood,
    What long, what longer hours, one lifelong night,
Ere ye again, who so in vain have wooed
    Your last hope lost, who so in vain invite
Your lips to that their unforgotten food,
    Ere ye, ere ye again shall see the light!

Alas! the bitter banks in Willowwood,
    With tear-spurge wan, with blood-wort burning red:
Alas! if ever such a pillow could
    Steep deep the soul in sleep till she were dead,—
Better all life forget her than this thing,
That Willowwood should hold her wandering!"

So sang he: and as meeting rose and rose
   Together cling through the wind's wellaway
   Nor change at once, yet near the end of day
The leaves drop loosened where the heart-stain glows,—
So when the song died did the kiss unclose;
   And her face fell back drowned, and was as grey
   As its grey eyes; and if it ever may
Meet mine again I know not if Love knows.

Only I know that I leaned low and drank
A long draught from the water where she sank,
   Her breath and all her tears and all her soul:
And as I leaned, I know I felt Love's face
Pressed on my neck with moan of pity and grace,
   Till both our heads were in his aureole.

SONNET LIII   WITHOUT HER

What of her glass without her? The blank grey
   There where the pool is blind of the moon's face.
   Her dress without her? The tossed empty space
Of cloud-rack whence the moon has passed away.
Her paths without her? Day's appointed sway
   Usurped by desolate night. Her pillowed place
   Without her? Tears, ah me! for love's good grace,
And cold forgetfulness of night or day.

What of the heart without her? Nay, poor heart,
   Of thee what word remains ere speech be still?
   A wayfarer by barren ways and chill,
Steep ways and weary, without her thou art,
Where the long cloud, the long wood's counterpart,
   Sheds doubled darkness up the labouring hill.

Sweet Love,—but oh! most dread Desire of Love
 Life-thwarted. Linked in gyves I saw them stand,
 Love shackled with Vain-longing, hand to hand:
And one was eyed as the blue vault above:
But hope tempestuous like a fire-cloud hove
 I' the other's gaze, even as in his whose wand
 Vainly all night with spell-wrought power has spann'd
The unyielding caves of some deep treasure-trove.

Also his lips, two writhen flakes of flame,
 Made moan: "Alas O Love, thus leashed with me!
 Wing-footed thou, wing-shouldered, once born free:
And I, thy cowering self, in chains grown tame,—
Bound to thy body and soul, named with thy name,—
 Life's iron heart, even Love's Fatality."

SONNET LV   STILLBORN LOVE

The hour which might have been yet might not be,
 Which man's and woman's heart conceived and bore
 Yet whereof life was barren,—on what shore
Bides it the breaking of Time's weary sea?
Bondchild of all consummate joys set free,
 It somewhere sighs and serves, and mute before
 The house of Love, hears through the echoing door
His hours elect in choral consonancy.

But lo! what wedded souls now hand in hand
Together tread at last the immortal strand
 With eyes where burning memory lights love home?
Lo! how the little outcast hour has turned
And leaped to them and in their faces yearned:—
 "I am your child: O parents, ye have come!"

I. HERSELF

To be a sweetness more desired than Spring;
　　A bodily beauty more acceptable
　　Than the wild rose-tree's arch that crowns the fell;
To be an essence more environing
Than wine's drained juice; a music ravishing
　　More than the passionate pulse of Philomel;—
　　To be all this 'neath one soft bosom's swell
That is the flower of life:—how strange a thing!

How strange a thing to be what Man can know
　　But as a sacred secret! Heaven's own screen
Hides her soul's purest depth and loveliest glow;
　　Closely withheld, as all things most unseen,—
　　The wave-bowered pearl,—the heart-shaped seal of green
That flecks the snowdrop underneath the snow.

II. HER LOVE

She loves him; for her infinite soul is Love,
　　And he her lodestar. Passion in her is
　　A glass facing his fire, where the bright bliss
Is mirrored, and the heat returned. Yet move
That glass, a stranger's amorous flame to prove,
　　And it shall turn, by instant contraries,
　　Ice to the moon; while her pure fire to his
For whom it burns, clings close i' the heart's alcove.

Lo! they are one. With wifely breast to breast
　　And circling arms, she welcomes all command
　　Of love,—her soul to answering ardours fann'd:
Yet as morn springs or twilight sinks to rest,
Ah! who shall say she deems not loveliest
　　The hour of sisterly sweet hand-in-hand?

If to grow old in Heaven is to grow young,
  (As the Seer saw and said,) then blest were he
  With youth for evermore, whose heaven should be
True Woman, she whom these weak notes have sung.
Here and hereafter,—choir-strains of her tongue,—
  Sky-spaces of her eyes,—sweet signs that flee
  About her soul's immediate sanctuary,—
Were Paradise all uttermost worlds among.

The sunrise blooms and withers on the hill
  Like any hillflower; and the noblest troth
  Dies here to dust. Yet shall Heaven's promise clothe
Even yet those lovers who have cherished still
This test for love:—in every kiss sealed fast
To feel the first kiss and forebode the last.

SONNET LIX   LOVE'S LAST GIFT

Love to his singer held a glistening leaf,
  And said: "The rose-tree and the apple-tree
  Have fruits to vaunt or flowers to lure the bee;
And golden shafts are in the feathered sheaf
Of the great harvest-marshal, the year's chief,
  Victorious Summer; aye, and 'neath warm sea
  Strange secret grasses lurk inviolably
Between the filtering channels of sunk reef.

"All are my blooms; and all sweet blooms of love
  To thee I gave while Spring and Summer sang;
  But Autumn stops to listen, with some pang
From those worse things the wind is moaning of.
Only this laurel dreads no winter days:
Take my last gift; thy heart hath sung my praise."

Part II. *Change and Fate*

◆ ◆ ◆ ◆ ◆

SONNET LX   TRANSFIGURED LIFE

As growth of form or momentary glance
    In a child's features will recall to mind
    The father's with the mother's face combin'd,—
Sweet interchange that memories still enhance:
And yet, as childhood's years and youth's advance,
    The gradual mouldings leave one stamp behind,
    Till in the blended likeness now we find
A separate man's or woman's countenance:—

So in the Song, the singer's Joy and Pain,
    Its very parents, evermore expand
To bid the passion's fullgrown birth remain,
    By Art's transfiguring essence subtly spann'd;
    And from that song-cloud shaped as a man's hand
There comes the sound as of abundant rain.

SONNET LXI   THE SONG-THROE

By thine own tears thy song must tears beget,
  O Singer! Magic mirror thou hast none
  Except thy manifest heart; and save thine own
Anguish or ardour, else no amulet.
Cisterned in Pride, verse is the feathery jet
  Of soulless air-flung fountains; nay, more dry
  Than the Dead Sea for throats that thirst and sigh,
That song o'er which no singer's lids grew wet.

The Song-god—He the Sun-god—is no slave
  Of thine: thy Hunter he, who for thy soul
  Fledges his shaft: to no august control
Of thy skilled hand his quivered store he gave:
But if thy lips' loud cry leap to his smart,
The inspir'd recoil shall pierce thy brother's heart.

SONNET LXII   THE SOUL'S SPHERE

Some prisoned moon in steep cloud-fastnesses,—
  Throned queen and thralled; some dying sun whose pyre
  Blazed with momentous memorable fire;—
Who hath not yearned and fed his heart with these?
Who, sleepless, hath not anguished to appease
  Tragical shadow's realm of sound and sight
  Conjectured in the lamentable night? . . .
Lo! the soul's sphere of infinite images!

What sense shall count them? Whether it forecast
  The rose-winged hours that flutter in the van
  Of Love's unquestioning unrevealèd span,—
Visions of golden futures: or that last
Wild pageant of the accumulated past
  That clangs and flashes for a drowning man.

SONNET LXIII   INCLUSIVENESS

The changing guests, each in a different mood,
   Sit at the roadside table and arise:
   And every life among them in like wise
Is a soul's board set daily with new food.
What man has bent o'er his son's sleep, to brood
   How that face shall watch his when cold it lies?—
   Or thought, as his own mother kissed his eyes,
Of what her kiss was when his father wooed?

May not this ancient room thou sitt'st in dwell
   In separate living souls for joy or pain?
   Nay, all its corners may be painted plain
Where Heaven shows pictures of some life spent well;
   And may be stamped, a memory all in vain,
Upon the sight of lidless eyes in Hell.

SONNET LXIV   ARDOUR AND MEMORY

The cuckoo-throb, the heartbeat of the Spring;
   The rosebud's blush that leaves it as it grows
   Into the full-eyed fair unblushing rose;
The summer clouds that visit every wing
With fires of sunrise and of sunsetting;
   The furtive flickering streams to light re-born
   'Mid airs new-fledged and valorous lusts of morn,
While all the daughters of the daybreak sing:—

These ardour loves, and memory: and when flown
   All joys, and through dark forest-boughs in flight
   The wind swoops onward brandishing the light,
Even yet the rose-tree's verdure left alone
Will flush all ruddy though the rose be gone;
   With ditties and with dirges infinite.

SONNET LXV   KNOWN IN VAIN

As two whose love, first foolish, widening scope,
   Knows suddenly, to music high and soft,
   The Holy of holies; who because they scoff'd
Are now amazed with shame, nor dare to cope
With the whole truth aloud, lest heaven should ope;
   Yet, at their meetings, laugh not as they laugh'd
   In speech; nor speak, at length; but sitting oft
Together, within hopeless sight of hope
For hours are silent:—So it happeneth
   When Work and Will awake too late, to gaze
After their life sailed by, and hold their breath.
   Ah! who shall dare to search through what sad maze
   Thenceforth their incommunicable ways
Follow the desultory feet of Death?

SONNET LXVI   THE HEART OF THE NIGHT

From child to youth; from youth to arduous man;
   From lethargy to fever of the heart;
   From faithful life to dream-dowered days apart;
From trust to doubt; from doubt to brink of ban;—
Thus much of change in one swift cycle ran
   Till now. Alas, the soul!—how soon must she
   Accept her primal immortality,—
The flesh resume its dust whence it began?

O Lord of work and peace! O Lord of life!
   O Lord, the awful Lord of will! though late,
     Even yet renew this soul with duteous breath:
That when the peace is garnered in from strife,
   The work retrieved, the will regenerate,
     This soul may see thy face, O Lord of death!

SONNET LXVII   THE LANDMARK

Was *that* the landmark? What,—the foolish well
   Whose wave, low down, I did not stoop to drink,
   But sat and flung the pebbles from its brink
In sport to send its imaged skies pell-mell,
(And mine own image, had I noted well!)—
   Was that my point of turning?—I had thought
   The stations of my course should rise unsought,
As altar-stone or ensigned citadel.

But lo! the path is missed, I must go back,
   And thirst to drink when next I reach the spring
Which once I stained, which since may have grown black.
   Yet though no light be left nor bird now sing
   As here I turn, I'll thank God, hastening,
That the same goal is still on the same track.

SONNET LXVIII   A DARK DAY

The gloom that breathes upon me with these airs
   Is like the drops which strike the traveller's brow
   Who knows not, darkling, if they bring him now
Fresh storm, or be old rain the covert bears.
Ah! bodes this hour some harvest of new tares,
   Or hath but memory of the day whose plough
   Sowed hunger once,—the night at length when thou,
O prayer found vain, didst fall from out my prayers?

How prickly were the growths which yet how smooth,
   Along the hedgerows of this journey shed,
Lie by Time's grace till night and sleep may soothe!
   Even as the thistledown from pathsides dead
Gleaned by a girl in autumns of her youth,
   Which one new year makes soft her marriage-bed.

SONNET LXIX   AUTUMN IDLENESS

This sunlight shames November where he grieves
   In dead red leaves, and will not let him shun
    The day, though bough with bough be over-run.
But with a blessing every glade receives
High salutation; while from hillock-eaves
   The deer gaze calling, dappled white and dun,
    As if, being foresters of old, the sun
Had marked them with the shade of forest-leaves.

Here dawn to-day unveiled her magic glass;
   Here noon now gives the thirst and takes the dew;
Till eve bring rest when other good things pass.
   And here the lost hours the lost hours renew
While I still lead my shadow o'er the grass,
   Nor know, for longing, that which I should do.

SONNET LXX   THE HILL SUMMIT

This feast-day of the sun, his altar there
   In the broad west has blazed for vesper-song;
   And I have loitered in the vale too long
And gaze now a belated worshipper.
Yet may I not forget that I was 'ware,
   So journeying, of his face at intervals
   Transfigured where the fringed horizon falls,—
A fiery bush with coruscating hair.

And now that I have climbed and won this height,
   I must tread downward through the sloping shade
And travel the bewildered tracks till night.
   Yet for this hour I still may here be stayed
   And see the gold air and the silver fade
And the last bird fly into the last light.

I

Eat thou and drink; to-morrow thou shalt die.
  Surely the earth, that's wise being very old,
  Needs not our help. Then loose me, love, and hold
Thy sultry hair up from my face; that I
May pour for thee this golden wine, brim-high,
  Till round the glass thy fingers glow like gold.
  We'll drown all hours: thy song, while hours are toll'd,
Shall leap, as fountains veil the changing sky.

Now kiss, and think that there are really those,
  My own high-bosomed beauty, who increase
    Vain gold, vain lore, and yet might choose our way!
    Through many years they toil; then on a day
  They die not,—for their life was death,—but cease;
And round their narrow lips the mould falls close.

II

Watch thou and fear; to-morrow thou shalt die.
  Or art thou sure thou shalt have time for death?
  Is not the day which God's word promiseth
To come man knows not when? In yonder sky,
Now while we speak, the sun speeds forth: can I
  Or thou assure him of his goal? God's breath
  Even at this moment haply quickeneth
The air to a flame; till spirits, always nigh
Though screened and hid, shall walk the daylight here.
  And dost thou prate of all that man shall do?
    Canst thou, who hast but plagues, presume to be
    Glad in his gladness that comes after thee?
  Will *his* strength slay *thy* worm in Hell? Go to:
Cover thy countenance, and watch, and fear.

III

Think thou and act; to-morrow thou shalt die.
   Outstretched in the sun's warmth upon the shore,
    Thou say'st: "Man's measured path is all gone o'er:
Up all his years, steeply, with strain and sigh,
Man clomb until he touched the truth; and I,
    Even I, am he whom it was destined for."
   How should this be? Art thou then so much more
Than they who sowed, that thou shouldst reap thereby?

Nay, come up hither. From this wave-washed mound
   Unto the furthest flood-brim look with me;
Then reach on with thy thought till it be drown'd.
   Miles and miles distant though the last line be,
And though thy soul sail leagues and leagues beyond,—
   Still, leagues beyond those leagues, there is more sea.

SONNETS LXXIV, LXXV, LXXVI   OLD AND NEW ART
I. ST. LUKE THE PAINTER

Give honour unto Luke Evangelist;
   For he it was (the aged legends say)
   Who first taught Art to fold her hands and pray.
Scarcely at once she dared to rend the mist
Of devious symbols: but soon having wist
   How sky-breadth and field-silence and this day
   Are symbols also in some deeper way,
She looked through these to God and was God's priest.

And if, past noon, her toil began to irk,
   And she sought talismans, and turned in vain
    To soulless self-reflections of man's skill,—
    Yet now, in this the twilight, she might still
   Kneel in the latter grass to pray again,
Ere the night cometh and she may not work.

II. NOT AS THESE

"I am not as these are," the poet saith
　　In youth's pride, and the painter, among men
　　At bay, where never pencil comes nor pen,
And shut about with his own frozen breath.
To others for whom only rhyme wins faith
　　As poets,—only paint as painters,—then
　　He turns in the cold silence; and again
Shrinking, "I am not as these are," he saith.

And say that this is so, what follows it?
　　For were thine eyes set backwards in thine head,
　　　　Such words were well; but they see on, and far.
Unto the lights of the great Past, new-lit
　　Fair for the Future's track, look thou instead,—
　　　　Say thou instead, "I am not as *these* are."

III. THE HUSBANDMEN

Though God, as one that is an householder,
　　Called these to labour in His vineyard first,
　　Before the husk of darkness was well burst
Bidding them grope their way out and bestir,
(Who, questioned of their wages, answered, "Sir,
　　Unto each man a penny:") though the worst
　　Burthen of heat was theirs and the dry thirst:
Though God has since found none such as these were
To do their work like them:—Because of this
　　Stand not ye idle in the market-place.
　　　　Which of ye knoweth *he* is not that last
Who may be first by faith and will?—yea, his
　　The hand which after the appointed days
　　　　And hours shall give a Future to their Past?

SONNET LXXVII SOUL'S BEAUTY

Under the arch of Life, where love and death,
　　Terror and mystery, guard her shrine, I saw
　　Beauty enthroned; and though her gaze struck awe,
I drew it in as simply as my breath.
Hers are the eyes which, over and beneath,
　　The sky and sea bend on thee,—which can draw,
　　By sea or sky or woman, to one law,
The allotted bondman of her palm and wreath.

This is that Lady Beauty, in whose praise
　　Thy voice and hand shake still,—long known to thee
　　　By flying hair and fluttering hem,—the beat
　　　Following her daily of thy heart and feet,
　　How passionately and irretrievably,
In what fond flight, how many ways and days!

SONNET LXXVIII BODY'S BEAUTY

Of Adam's first wife, Lilith, it is told
　　(The witch he loved before the gift of Eve,)
　　That, ere the snake's, her sweet tongue could deceive,
And her enchanted hair was the first gold.
And still she sits, young while the earth is old,
　　And, subtly of herself contemplative,
　　Draws men to watch the bright web she can weave,
Till heart and body and life are in its hold.

The rose and poppy are her flowers; for where
　　Is he not found, O Lilith, whom shed scent
And soft-shed kisses and soft sleep shall snare?
　　Lo! as that youth's eyes burned at thine, so went
　　Thy spell through him, and left his straight neck bent
And round his heart one strangling golden hair.

SONNET LXXIX   THE MONOCHORD

Is it this sky's vast vault or ocean's sound
    That is Life's self and draws my life from me,
    And by instinct ineffable decree
Holds my breath quailing on the bitter bound?
Nay, is it Life or Death, thus thunder-crown'd,
    That 'mid the tide of all emergency
    Now notes my separate wave, and to what sea
Its difficult eddies labour in the ground?

Oh! what is this that knows the road I came,
The flame turned cloud, the cloud returned to flame,
    The lifted shifted steeps and all the way?—
That draws round me at last this wind-warm space,
And in regenerate rapture turns my face
    Upon the devious coverts of dismay?

SONNET LXXX   FROM DAWN TO NOON

As the child knows not if his mother's face
    Be fair; nor of his elders yet can deem
    What each most is; but as of hill or stream
At dawn, all glimmering life surrounds his place:
Who yet, tow'rd noon of his half-weary race,
    Pausing awhile beneath the high sun-beam
    And gazing steadily back,—as through a dream,
In things long past new features now can trace:—

Even so the thought that is at length fullgrown
    Turns back to note the sun-smit paths, all grey
And marvellous once, where first it walked alone;
    And haply doubts, amid the unblenching day,
    Which most or least impelled its onward way,—
Those unknown things or these things overknown.

What place so strange,—though unrevealèd snow
   With unimaginable fires arise
   At the earth's end,—what passion of surprise
Like frost-bound fire-girt scenes of long ago?
Lo! this is none but I this hour; and lo!
   This is the very place which to mine eyes
   Those mortal hours in vain immortalize,
'Mid hurrying crowds, with what alone I know.

City, of thine a single simple door,
   By some new Power reduplicate, must be
   Even yet my life-porch in eternity,
Even with one presence filled, as once of yore:
Or mocking winds whirl round a chaff-strown floor
   Thee and thy years and these my words and me.

I said: "Nay, pluck not,—let the first fruit be:
   Even as thou sayest, it is sweet and red,
   But let it ripen still. The tree's bent head
Sees in the stream its own fecundity
And bides the day of fulness. Shall not we
   At the sun's hour that day possess the shade,
   And claim our fruit before its ripeness fade,
And eat it from the branch and praise the tree?"

I say: "Alas! our fruit hath wooed the sun
   Too long,—'tis fallen and floats adown the stream.
Lo, the last clusters! Pluck them every one,
   And let us sup with summer; ere the gleam
Of autumn set the year's pent sorrow free,
And the woods wail like echoes from the sea."

SONNET LXXXIII BARREN SPRING

Once more the changed year's turning wheel returns:
    And as a girl sails balanced in the wind,
    And now before and now again behind
Stoops as it swoops, with cheek that laughs and burns,—
So Spring comes merry towards me here, but earns
    No answering smile from me, whose life is twin'd
    With the dead boughs that winter still must bind,
And whom to-day the Spring no more concerns.

Behold, this crocus is a withering flame;
    This snowdrop, snow; this apple-blossom's part
    To breed the fruit that breeds the serpent's art.
Nay, for these Spring-flowers, turn thy face from them,
Nor stay till on the year's last lily-stem
    The white cup shrivels round the golden heart.

SONNET LXXXIV FAREWELL TO THE GLEN

Sweet stream-fed glen, why say "farewell" to thee
    Who far'st so well and find'st for ever smooth
    The brow of Time where man may read no ruth?
Nay, do thou rather say "farewell" to me,
Who now fare forth in bitterer fantasy
    Than erst was mine where other shade might soothe
    By other streams, what while in fragrant youth
The bliss of being sad made melancholy.

And yet, farewell! For better shalt thou fare
    When children bathe sweet faces in thy flow
And happy lovers blend sweet shadows there
    In hours to come, than when an hour ago
Thine echoes had but one man's sighs to bear
    And thy trees whispered what he feared to know.

SONNET LXXXV   VAIN VIRTUES

What is the sorriest thing that enters Hell?
　None of the sins,—but this and that fair deed
　Which a soul's sin at length could supersede.
These yet are virgins, whom death's timely knell
Might once have sainted; whom the fiends compel
　Together now, in snake-bound shuddering sheaves
　Of anguish, while the pit's pollution leaves
Their refuse maidenhood abominable.

Night sucks them down, the tribute of the pit,
　Whose names, half entered in the book of Life,
　Were God's desire at noon. And as their hair
And eyes sink last, the Torturer deigns no whit
　To gaze, but, yearning, waits his destined wife,
　The Sin still blithe on earth that sent them there.

SONNET LXXXVI   LOST DAYS

The lost days of my life until to-day,
　What were they, could I see them on the street
　Lie as they fell? Would they be ears of wheat
Sown once for food but trodden into clay?
Or golden coins squandered and still to pay?
　Or drops of blood dabbling the guilty feet?
　Or such spilt water as in dreams must cheat
The undying throats of Hell, athirst alway?

I do not see them here; but after death
　God knows I know the faces I shall see,
Each one a murdered self, with low last breath.
　"I am thyself,—what hast thou done to me?"
"And I—and I—thyself," (lo! each one saith,)
　"And thou thyself to all eternity!"

When first that horse, within whose populous womb
   The birth was death, o'ershadowed Troy with fate,
   Her elders, dubious of its Grecian freight,
Brought Helen there to sing the songs of home;
She whispered, "Friends, I am alone; come, come!"
   Then, crouched within, Ulysses waxed afraid,
   And on his comrades' quivering mouths he laid
His hands, and held them till the voice was dumb.

The same was he who, lashed to his own mast,
   There where the sea-flowers screen the charnel-caves,
Beside the sirens' singing island pass'd,
   Till sweetness failed along the inveterate waves. . . .
Say, soul,—are songs of Death no heaven to thee,
Nor shames her lip the cheek of Victory?

SONNET LXXXVIII   HERO'S LAMP*

That lamp thou fill'st in Eros' name to-night,
   O Hero, shall the Sestian augurs take
   To-morrow, and for drowned Leander's sake
To Anteros its fireless lip shall plight.
Aye, waft the unspoken vow: yet dawn's first light
   On ebbing storm and life twice ebb'd must break;
   While 'neath no sunrise, by the Avernian Lake,
Lo where Love walks, Death's pallid neophyte.

That lamp within Anteros' shadowy shrine
   Shall stand unlit (for so the gods decree)
   Till some one man the happy issue see
Of a life's love, and bid its flame to shine:
Which still may rest unfir'd; for, theirs or thine,
   O brother, what brought love to them or thee?

SONNET LXXXIX   THE TREES OF THE GARDEN

Ye who have passed Death's haggard hills; and ye
   Whom trees that knew your sires shall cease to know
   And still stand silent:—is it all a show,—
A wisp that laughs upon the wall?—decree
Of some inexorable supremacy
   Which ever, as man strains his blind surmise
   From depth to ominous depth, looks past his eyes,
Sphinx-faced with unabashèd augury?

Nay, rather question the Earth's self. Invoke
   The storm-felled forest trees moss-grown to-day
   Whose roots are hillocks where the children play;
Or ask the silver sapling 'neath what yoke
Those stars, his spray-crown's clustering gems, shall wage
Their journey still when his boughs shrink with age.

SONNET XC   "RETRO ME, SATHANA!"

Get thee behind me. Even as, heavy-curled,
   Stooping against the wind, a charioteer
   Is snatched from out his chariot by the hair,
So shall Time be; and as the void car, hurled
   Abroad by reinless steeds, even so the world:
   Yea, even as chariot-dust upon the air,
   It shall be sought and not found anywhere.
Get thee behind me, Satan. Oft unfurled,
Thy perilous wings can beat and break like lath
   Much mightiness of men to win thee praise.
   Leave these weak feet to tread in narrow ways.
Thou still, upon the broad vine-sheltered path,
Mayst wait the turning of the phials of wrath
   For certain years, for certain months and days.

As when two men have loved a woman well,
    Each hating each, through Love's and Death's deceit;
    Since not for either this stark marriage-sheet
And the long pauses of this wedding-bell;
Yet o'er her grave the night and day dispel
    At last their feud forlorn, with cold and heat;
    Nor other than dear friends to death may fleet
The two lives left that most of her can tell:—

So separate hopes, which in a soul had wooed
    The one same Peace, strove with each other long,
    And Peace before their faces perished since:
So through that soul, in restless brotherhood,
    They roam together now, and wind among
    Its bye-streets, knocking at the dusty inns.

SONNETS XCII, XCIII   THE SUN'S SHAME

I

Beholding youth and hope in mockery caught
    From life; and mocking pulses that remain
    When the soul's death of bodily death is fain;
Honour unknown, and honour known unsought;
And penury's sedulous self-torturing thought
    On gold, whose master therewith buys his bane;
    And longed-for woman longing all in vain
For lonely man with love's desire distraught;
And wealth, and strength, and power, and pleasantness,
    Given unto bodies of whose souls men say,
    None poor and weak, slavish and foul, as they:—
Beholding these things, I behold no less
The blushing morn and blushing eve confess
    The shame that loads the intolerable day.

As some true chief of men, bowed down with stress
 Of life's disastrous eld, on blossoming youth
 May gaze, and murmur with self-pity and ruth,—
"Might I thy fruitless treasure but possess,
Such blessing of mine all coming years should bless;"—
 Then sends one sigh forth to the unknown goal,
 And bitterly feels breathe against his soul
The hour swift-winged of nearer nothingness:—

Even so the World's grey Soul to the green World
 Perchance one hour must cry: "Woe's me, for whom
 Inveteracy of ill portends the doom,—
Whose heart's old fire in shadow of shame is furl'd:
While thou even as of yore art journeying,
All soulless now, yet merry with the Spring!"

SONNET XCIV   MICHELANGELO'S KISS

Great Michelangelo, with age grown bleak
 And uttermost labours, having once o'ersaid
 All grievous memories on his long life shed,
This worst regret to one true heart could speak:—
That when, with sorrowing love and reverence meek,
 He stooped o'er sweet Colonna's dying bed,
 His Muse and dominant Lady, spirit-wed,—
Her hand he kissed, but not her brow or cheek.

O Buonarruoti,—good at Art's fire-wheels
 To urge her chariot!—even thus the Soul,
 Touching at length some sorely-chastened goal,
Earns oftenest but a little: her appeals
Were deep and mute,—lowly her claim. Let be:
What holds for her Death's garner? And for thee?

SONNET XCV   THE VASE OF LIFE

Around the vase of Life at your slow pace
   He has not crept, but turned it with his hands,
   And all its sides already understands.
There, girt, one breathes alert for some great race;
Whose road runs far by sands and fruitful space;
   Who laughs, yet through the jolly throng has pass'd;
   Who weeps, nor stays for weeping; who at last,
A youth, stands somewhere crowned, with silent face.

And he has filled this vase with wine for blood,
   With blood for tears, with spice for burning vow,
    With watered flowers for buried love most fit;
And would have cast it shattered to the flood,
   Yet in Fate's name has kept it whole; which now
    Stands empty till his ashes fall in it.

SONNET XCVI   LIFE THE BELOVED

As thy friend's face, with shadow of soul o'erspread,
   Somewhile unto thy sight perchance hath been
   Ghastly and strange, yet never so is seen
In thought, but to all fortunate favour wed;
As thy love's death-bound features never dead
   To memory's glass return, but contravene
   Frail fugitive days, and alway keep, I ween,
Than all new life a livelier lovelihead:—

So Life herself, thy spirit's friend and love,
   Even still as Spring's authentic harbinger
    Glows with fresh hours for hope to glorify;
Though pale she lay when in the winter grove
   Her funeral flowers were snow-flakes shed on her
    And the red wings of frost-fire rent the sky.

SONNET XCVII   A SUPERSCRIPTION

Look in my face; my name is Might-have-been;
  I am also called No-more, Too-late, Farewell;
  Unto thine ear I hold the dead-sea shell
Cast up thy Life's foam-fretted feet between;
Unto thine eyes the glass where that is seen
  Which had Life's form and Love's, but by my spell
  Is now a shaken shadow intolerable,
Of ultimate things unuttered the frail screen.

Mark me, how still I am! But should there dart
  One moment through thy soul the soft surprise
  Of that winged Peace which lulls the breath of sighs,—
Then shalt thou see me smile, and turn apart
Thy visage to mine ambush at thy heart
  Sleepless with cold commemorative eyes.

SONNET XCVIII   HE AND I

Whence came his feet into my field, and why?
  How is it that he sees it all so drear?
  How do I see his seeing, and how hear
The name his bitter silence knows it by?
This was the little fold of separate sky
  Whose pasturing clouds in the soul's atmosphere
  Drew living light from one continual year:
How should he find it lifeless? He, or I?

Lo! this new Self now wanders round my field,
  With plaints for every flower, and for each tree
  A moan, the sighing wind's auxiliary:
And o'er sweet waters of my life, that yield
Unto his lips no draught but tears unseal'd,
  Even in my place he weeps. Even I, not he.

I

To-day Death seems to me an infant child
    Which her worn mother Life upon my knee
    Has set to grow my friend and play with me;
If haply so my heart might be beguil'd
To find no terrors in a face so mild,—
    If haply so my weary heart might be
    Unto the newborn milky eyes of thee,
O Death, before resentment reconcil'd.

How long, O Death? And shall thy feet depart
    Still a young child's with mine, or wilt thou stand
Fullgrown the helpful daughter of my heart,
    What time with thee indeed I reach the strand
Of the pale wave which knows thee what thou art,
    And drink it in the hollow of thy hand?

II

And thou, O Life, the lady of all bliss,
    With whom, when our first heart beat full and fast,
    I wandered till the haunts of men were pass'd,
And in fair places found all bowers amiss
Till only woods and waves might hear our kiss,
    While to the winds all thought of Death we cast:—
    Ah, Life! and must I have from thee at last
No smile to greet me and no babe but this?

Lo! Love, the child once ours; and Song, whose hair
    Blew like a flame and blossomed like a wreath;
And Art, whose eyes were worlds by God found fair:
    These o'er the book of Nature mixed their breath
With neck-twined arms, as oft we watched them there:
    And did these die that thou mightst bear me Death?

When vain desire at last and vain regret
   Go hand in hand to death, and all is vain,
   What shall assuage the unforgotten pain
And teach the unforgetful to forget?
Shall Peace be still a sunk stream long unmet,—
   Or may the soul at once in a green plain
   Stoop through the spray of some sweet life-fountain
And cull the dew-drenched flowering amulet?

Ah! when the wan soul in that golden air
   Between the scriptured petals softly blown
   Peers breathless for the gift of grace unknown,—
Ah! let none other alien spell soe'er
But only the one Hope's one name be there,—
   Not less nor more, but even that word alone.

*SONNET LXXXVIII   HERO'S LAMP: *After the deaths of Leander and of Hero, the signal-lamp was dedicated to Anterca, with the edict that no man should light it unless his love had proved fortunate.*

Eden Bower

It was Lilith the wife of Adam:
                 (*Sing Eden Bower!*)
Not a drop of her blood was human,
But she was made like a soft sweet woman.

Lilith stood on the skirts of Eden;
                 (*Alas the hour!*)
She was the first that thence was driven;
With her was hell and with Eve was heaven.

In the ear of the Snake said Lilith:—

(*Sing Eden Bower!*)

"To thee I come when the rest is over;
A snake was I when thou wast my lover.

"I was the fairest snake in Eden:

(*Alas the hour!*)

By the earth's will, new form and feature
Made me a wife for the earth's new creature.

"Take me thou as I come from Adam:

(*Sing Eden Bower!*)

Once again shall my love subdue thee;
The past is past and I am come to thee.

"O but Adam was thrall to Lilith!

(*Alas the hour!*)

All the threads of my hair are golden,
And there in a net his heart was holden.

"O and Lilith was queen of Adam!

(*Sing Eden Bower!*)

All the day and the night together
My breath could shake his soul like a feather.

"What great joys had Adam and Lilith!—

(*Alas the hour!*)

Sweet close rings of the serpent's twining,
As heart in heart lay sighing and pining.

"What bright babes had Lilith and Adam!

(*Sing Eden Bower!*)

Shapes that coiled in the woods and waters,
Glittering sons and radiant daughters.

"O thou God, the Lord God of Eden!
                    (*Alas the hour!*)
Say, was this fair body for no man,
That of Adam's flesh thou mak'st him a woman?

"O thou Snake, the King-snake of Eden!
                    (*Sing Eden Bower!*)
God's strong will our necks are under,
But thou and I may cleave it in sunder.

"Help, sweet Snake, sweet lover of Lilith!
                    (*Alas the hour!*)
And let God learn how I loved and hated
Man in the image of God created.

"Help me once against Eve and Adam!
                    (*Sing Eden Bower!*)
Help me once for this one endeavour,
And then my love shall be thine for ever!

"Strong is God, the fell foe of Lilith:
                    (*Alas the hour!*)
Nought in heaven or earth may affright Him;
But join thou with me and we will smite Him.

"Strong is God, the great God of Eden:
                    (*Sing Eden Bower!*)
Over all He made He hath power;
But lend me thou thy shape for an hour!

"Lend thy shape for the love of Lilith!
                    (*Alas the hour!*)
Look, my mouth and my cheek are ruddy,
And thou art cold, and fire is my body.

"Lend thy shape for the hate of Adam!
               (*Sing Eden Bower!*)
That he may wail my joy that forsook him,
And curse the day when the bride-sleep took him.

"Lend thy shape for the shame of Eden!
               (*Alas the hour!*)
Is not the foe-God weak as the foeman
When love grows hate in the heart of a woman?

"Wouldst thou know the heart's hope of Lilith?
               (*Sing Eden Bower!*)
Then bring thou close thine head till it glisten
Along my breast, and lip me and listen.

"Am I sweet, O sweet Snake of Eden?
               (*Alas the hour!*)
Then ope thine ear to my warm mouth's cooing
And learn what deed remains for our doing.

"Thou didst hear when God said to Adam:—
               (*Sing Eden Bower!*)
'Of all this wealth I have made thee warden;
Thou'rt free to eat of the trees of the garden:

"'Only of one tree eat not in Eden:
               (*Alas the hour!*)
All save one I give to thy freewill,—
The Tree of the Knowledge of Good and Evil.'

"O my love, come nearer to Lilith!
               (*Sing Eden Bower!*)
In thy sweet folds bind me and bend me,
And let me feel the shape thou shalt lend me.

"In thy shape I'll go back to Eden;
                    (*Alas the hour!*)
In these coils that Tree will I grapple,
And stretch this crowned head forth by the apple.

"Lo, Eve bends to the breath of Lilith!
                    (*Sing Eden Bower!*)
O how then shall my heart desire
All her blood as food to its fire!

"Lo, Eve bends to the words of Lilith!—
                    (*Alas the hour!*)
'Nay, this Tree's fruit,—why should ye hate it,
Or Death be born the day that ye ate it?

" 'Nay, but on that great day in Eden,
                    (*Sing Eden Bower!*)
By the help that in this wise Tree is,
God knows well ye shall be as He is.'

"Then Eve shall eat and give unto Adam;
                    (*Alas the hour!*)
And then they both shall know they are naked,
And their hearts ache as my heart hath achèd.

"Ay, let them hide 'mid the trees of Eden,
                    (*Sing Eden Bower!*)
As in the cool of the day in the garden
God shall walk without pity or pardon.

"Hear, thou Eve, the man's heart in Adam!
                    (*Alas the hour!*)
Of his brave words hark to the bravest:—
'This the woman gave that thou gavest.'

"Hear Eve speak, yea list to her, Lilith!
           (Sing Eden Bower!)
Feast thine heart with words that shall sate it—
'This the serpent gave and I ate it.'

"O proud Eve, cling close to thine Adam,
           (Alas the hour!)
Driven forth as the beasts of his naming
By the sword that for ever is flaming.

"Know, thy path is known unto Lilith!
           (Sing Eden Bower!)
While the blithe birds sang at thy wedding,
There her tears grew thorns for thy treading.

"O my love, thou Love-snake of Eden!
           (Alas the hour!)
O to-day and the day to come after!
Loose me, love,—give breath to my laughter.

"O bright Snake, the Death-worm of Adam!
           (Sing Eden Bower!)
Wreathe thy neck with my hair's bright tether,
And wear my gold and thy gold together!

"On that day on the skirts of Eden,
           (Alas the hour!)
In thy shape shall I glide back to thee,
And in my shape for an instant view thee.

"But when thou'rt thou and Lilith is Lilith,
           (Sing Eden Bower!)
In what bliss past hearing or seeing
Shall each one drink of the other's being!

"With cries of 'Eve!' and 'Eden!' and 'Adam!'
                    (*Alas the hour!*)
How shall we mingle our love's caresses,
I in thy coils, and thou in my tresses!

"With those names, ye echoes of Eden,
                    (*Sing Eden Bower!*)
Fire shall cry from my heart that burneth,—
'Dust he is and to dust returneth!'

"Yet to-day, thou master of Lilith,—
                    (*Alas the hour!*)
Wrap me round in the form I'll borrow
And let me tell thee of sweet to-morrow.

"In the planted garden eastward in Eden,
                    (*Sing Eden Bower!*)
Where the river goes forth to water the garden,
The springs shall dry and the soil shall harden.

"Yea, where the bride-sleep fell upon Adam,
                    (*Alas the hour!*)
None shall hear when the storm-wind whistles
Through roses choked among thorns and thistles.

"Yea, beside the east-gate of Eden,
                    (*Sing Eden Bower!*)
Where God joined them and none might sever,
The sword turns this way and that for ever.

"What of Adam cast out of Eden?
                    (*Alas the hour!*)
Lo! with care like a shadow shaken,
He tills the hard earth whence he was taken.

"What of Eve too, cast out of Eden?
                    (*Sing Eden Bower!*)
Nay, but she, the bride of God's giving,
Must yet be mother of all men living.

"Lo, God's grace, by the grace of Lilith!
                    (*Alas the hour!*)
To Eve's womb, from our sweet to-morrow,
God shall greatly multiply sorrow.

"Fold me fast, O God-snake of Eden!
                    (*Sing Eden Bower!*)
What more prize than love to impel thee?
Grip and lip my limbs as I tell thee!

"Lo! two babes for Eve and for Adam!
                    (*Alas the hour!*)
Lo! sweet Snake, the travail and treasure,—
Two men-children born for their pleasure!

"The first is Cain and the second Abel:
                    (*Sing Eden Bower!*)
The soul of one shall be made thy brother,
And thy tongue shall lap the blood of the other."
                    (*Alas the hour!*)

The Stream's Secret

    What thing unto mine ear
    Wouldst thou convey,—what secret thing,
O wandering water ever whispering?
    Surely thy speech shall be of her.
Thou water, O thou whispering wanderer,
    What message dost thou bring?

Say, hath not Love leaned low
This hour beside thy far well-head,
And there through jealous hollowed fingers said
The thing that most I long to know,—
Murmuring with curls all dabbled in thy flow
And washed lips rosy red?

He told it to thee there
Where thy voice hath a louder tone;
But where it welters to this little moan
His will decrees that I should hear.
Now speak: for with the silence is no fear,
And I am all alone.

Shall Time not still endow
One hour with life, and I and she
Slake in one kiss the thirst of memory?
Say, stream; lest Love should disavow
Thy service, and the bird upon the bough
Sing first to tell it me.

What whisperest thou? Nay, why
Name the dead hours? I mind them well:
Their ghosts in many darkened doorways dwell
With desolate eyes to know them by.
The hour that must be born ere it can die,—
Of that I'd have thee tell.

But hear, before thou speak!
Withhold, I pray, the vain behest
That while the maze hath still its bower for quest
My burning heart should cease to seek.
Be sure that Love ordained for souls more meek
His roadside dells of rest.

Stream, when this silver thread
In flood-time is a torrent brown
May any bulwark bind thy foaming crown?
Shall not the waters surge and spread
And to the crannied boulders of their bed
Still shoot the dead drift down?

Let no rebuke find place
In speech of thine: or it shall prove
That thou dost ill expound the words of Love,
Even as thine eddy's rippling race
Would blur the perfect image of his face.
I will have none thereof.

O learn and understand
That 'gainst the wrongs himself did wreak
Love sought her aid; until her shadowy cheek
And eyes beseeching gave command;
And compassed in her close compassionate hand
My heart must burn and speak.

For then at last we spoke
What eyes so oft had told to eyes
Through that long-lingering silence whose half-sighs
Alone the buried secret broke,
Which with snatched hands and lips' reverberate stroke
Then from the heart did rise.

But she is far away
Now; nor the hours of night grown hoar
Bring yet to me, long gazing from the door,
The wind-stirred robe of roseate grey
And rose-crown of the hour that leads the day
When we shall meet once more.

Dark as thy blinded wave
        When brimming midnight floods the glen,—
Bright as the laughter of thy runnels when
        The dawn yields all the light they crave;
Even so these hours to wound and that to save
        Are sisters in Love's ken.

        Oh sweet her bending grace
        Then when I kneel beside her feet;
And sweet her eyes' o'erhanging heaven; and sweet
        The gathering folds of her embrace;
And her fall'n hair at last shed round my face
        When breaths and tears shall meet.

        Beneath her sheltering hair,
        In the warm silence near her breast,
Our kisses and our sobs shall sink to rest;
        As in some still trance made aware
That day and night have wrought to fulness there
        And Love has built our nest.

        And as in the dim grove,
        When the rains cease that hushed them long,
'Mid glistening boughs the song-birds wake to song,—
        So from our hearts deep-shrined in love,
While the leaves throb beneath, around, above,
        The quivering notes shall throng.

        Till tenderest words found vain
        Draw back to wonder mute and deep,
And closed lips in closed arms a silence keep,
        Subdued by memory's circling strain,—
The wind-rapt sound that the wind brings again
        While all the willows weep.

Then by her summoning art
Shall memory conjure back the sere
Autumnal Springs, from many a dying year
Born dead; and, bitter to the heart,
The very ways where now we walk apart
Who then shall cling so near.

And with each thought new-grown,
Some sweet caress or some sweet name
Low-breathed shall let me know her thought the same;
Making me rich with every tone
And touch of the dear heaven so long unknown
That filled my dreams with flame.

Pity and love shall burn
In her pressed cheek and cherishing hands;
And from the living spirit of love that stands
Between her lips to soothe and yearn,
Each separate breath shall clasp me round in turn
And loose my spirit's bands.

Oh passing sweet and dear,
Then when the worshipped form and face
Are felt at length in darkling close embrace;
Round which so oft the sun shone clear,
With mocking light and pitiless atmosphere,
In many an hour and place.

Ah me! with what proud growth
Shall that hour's thirsting race be run;
While, for each several sweetness still begun
Afresh, endures love's endless drouth:
Sweet hands, sweet hair, sweet cheeks, sweet eyes, sweet mouth,
Each singly wooed and won.

Yet most with the sweet soul
Shall love's espousals then be knit;
For very passion of peace shall breathe from it
O'er tremulous wings that touch the goal,
As on the unmeasured height of Love's control
The lustral fires are lit.

Therefore, when breast and cheek
Now part, from long embraces free,—
Each on the other gazing shall but see
A self that has no heed to speak:
All things unsought, yet nothing more to seek,—
One love in unity.

O water wandering past,—
Albeit to thee I speak this thing,
O water, thou that wanderest whispering,
Thou keep'st thy counsel to the last.
What spell upon thy bosom should Love cast,
His message thence to wring?

Nay, must thou hear the tale
Of the past days,—the heavy debt
Of life that obdurate time withholds,—ere yet
To win thine ear these prayers prevail,
And by thy voice Love's self with high All-hail
Yield up the amulet?

How should all this be told?—
All the sad sum of wayworn days;—
Heart's anguish in the impenetrable maze;
And on the waste uncoloured wold
The visible burthen of the sun grown cold
And the moon's labouring gaze?

Alas! shall hope be nurs'd
On life's all-succouring breast in vain,
And made so perfect only to be slain?
Or shall not rather the sweet thirst
Even yet rejoice the heart with warmth dispers'd
And strength grown fair again?

Stands it not by the door—
Love's Hour—till she and I shall meet;
With bodiless form and unapparent feet
That cast no shadow yet before,
Though round its head the dawn begins to pour
The breath that makes day sweet?

Its eyes invisible
Watch till the dial's thin-thrown shade
Be born,—yea, till the journeying line be laid
Upon the point that wakes the spell,
And there in lovelier light than tongue can tell
Its presence stand array'd.

Its soul remembers yet
Those sunless hours that passed it by;
And still it hears the night's disconsolate cry,
And feels the branches wringing wet
Cast on its brow, that may not once forget,
Dumb tears from the blind sky.

But oh! when now her foot
Draws near, for whose sake night and day
Were long in weary longing sighed away,—
The Hour of Love, 'mid airs grown mute,
Shall sing beside the door, and Love's own lute
Thrill to the passionate lay.

Thou know'st, for Love has told
Within thine ear, O stream, how soon
That song shall lift its sweet appointed tune.
O tell me, for my lips are cold,
And in my veins the blood is waxing old
Even while I beg the boon.

So, in that hour of sighs
Assuaged, shall we beside this stone
Yield thanks for grace; while in thy mirror shown
The twofold image softly lies,
Until we kiss, and each in other's eyes
Is imaged all alone.

Still silent? Can no art
Of Love's then move thy pity? Nay,
To thee let nothing come that owns his sway:
Let happy lovers have no part
With thee; nor even so sad and poor a heart
As thou hast spurned to-day.

To-day? Lo! night is here.
The glen grows heavy with some veil
Risen from the earth or fall'n to make earth pale;
And all stands hushed to eye and ear,
Until the night-wind shake the shade like fear
And every covert quail.

Ah! by a colder wave
On deathlier airs the hour must come
Which to thy heart, my love, shall call me home.
Between the lips of the low cave
Against that night the lapping waters lave,
And the dark lips are dumb.

But there Love's self doth stand,
   And with Life's weary wings far-flown,
And with Death's eyes that make the water moan,
   Gathers the water in his hand:
And they that drink know nought of sky or land
   But only love alone.

   O soul-sequestered face
   Far off,—O were that night but now!
So even beside that stream even I and thou
   Through thirsting lips should draw Love's grace,
And in the zone of that supreme embrace
   Bind aching breast and brow.

   O water whispering
   Still through the dark into mine ears,—
As with mine eyes, is it not now with hers?—
   Mine eyes that add to thy cold spring,
Wan water, wandering water weltering,
   This hidden tide of tears.

My Sister's Sleep

She fell asleep on Christmas Eve:
   At length the long-ungranted shade
   Of weary eyelids overweigh'd
The pain nought else might yet relieve.

Our mother, who had leaned all day
   Over the bed from chime to chime,
   Then raised herself for the first time,
And as she sat her down, did pray.

Her little work-table was spread
  With work to finish. For the glare
  Made by her candle, she had care
To work some distance from the bed.

Without, there was a cold moon up,
  Of winter radiance sheer and thin;
  The hollow halo it was in
Was like an icy crystal cup.

Through the small room, with subtle sound
  Of flame, by vents the fireshine drove
  And reddened. In its dim alcove
The mirror shed a clearness round.

I had been sitting up some nights,
  And my tired mind felt weak and blank;
  Like a sharp strengthening wine it drank
The stillness and the broken lights.

Twelve struck. That sound, by dwindling years
  Heard in each hour, crept off; and then
  The ruffled silence spread again,
Like water that a pebble stirs.

Our mother rose from where she sat:
  Her needles, as she laid them down,
  Met lightly, and her silken gown
Settled: no other noise than that.

"Glory unto the Newly Born!"
  So, as said angels, she did say;
  Because we were in Christmas Day,
Though it would still be long till morn.

Just then in the room over us
     There was a pushing back of chairs,
     As some who had sat unawares
So late, now heard the hour, and rose.

With anxious softly-stepping haste
     Our mother went where Margaret lay,
     Fearing the sounds o'erhead—should they
Have broken her long watched-for rest!

She stooped an instant, calm, and turned;
     But suddenly turned back again;
     And all her features seemed in pain
With woe, and her eyes gazed and yearned.

For my part, I but hid my face,
     And held my breath, and spoke no word:
     There was none spoken; but I heard
The silence for a little space.

Our mother bowed herself and wept:
     And both my arms fell, and I said,
     "God knows I knew that she was dead."
And there, all white, my sister slept.

Then kneeling, upon Christmas morn
     A little after twelve o'clock,
     We said, ere the first quarter struck,
"Christ's blessing on the newly born!"

For an Annunciation

EARLY GERMAN

The lilies stand before her like a screen
   Through which, upon this warm and solemn day,
   God surely hears. For there she kneels to pray
Who wafts our prayers to God—Mary the Queen
She was Faith's Present, parting what had been
   From what began with her, and is for aye.
   On either hand, God's twofold system lay:
With meek bowed face a Virgin prayed between.

So prays she, and the Dove flies in to her,
   And she has turned. At the low porch is one
     Who looks as though deep awe made him to smile.
Heavy with heat, the plants yield shadow there;
   The loud flies cross each other in the sun;
     And the aisled pillars meet the poplar-aisle.

The Portrait

This is her picture as she was:
   It seems a thing to wonder on,
As though mine image in the glass
   Should tarry when myself am gone.
I gaze until she seems to stir,—
Until mine eyes almost aver
   That now, even now, the sweet lips part
   To breathe the words of the sweet heart:—
And yet the earth is over her.

Alas! even such the thin-drawn ray
    That makes the prison-depths more rude,—
The drip of water night and day
    Giving a tongue to solitude.
Yet only this, of love's whole prize,
Remains; save what in mournful guise
    Takes counsel with my soul alone,—
    Save what is secret and unknown,
Below the earth, above the skies.

In painting her I shrined her face
    'Mid mystic trees, where light falls in
Hardly at all; a covert place
    Where you might think to find a din
Of doubtful talk, and a live flame
Wandering, and many a shape whose name
    Not itself knoweth, and old dew,
    And your own footsteps meeting you,
And all things going as they came.

A deep dim wood; and there she stands
    As in that wood that day: for so
Was the still movement of her hands
    And such the pure line's gracious flow.
And passing fair the type must seem,
Unknown the presence and the dream.
    'Tis she: though of herself, alas!
    Less than her shadow on the grass
Or than her image in the stream.

That day we met there, I and she
    One with the other all alone;
And we were blithe; yet memory
    Saddens those hours, as when the moon

Looks upon daylight. And with her
I stopped to drink the spring-water,
    Athirst where other waters sprang:
    And where the echo is, she sang,—
My soul another echo there.

But when that hour my soul won strength
    For words whose silence wastes and kills,
Dull raindrops smote us, and at length
    Thundered the heat within the hills.
That eve I spoke those words again
Beside the pelted window-pane;
    And there she hearkened what I said,
    With under-glances that surveyed
The empty pastures blind with rain.

Next day the memories of these things,
    Like leaves through which a bird has flown,
Still vibrated with Love's warm wings;
    Till I must make them all my own
And paint this picture. So, 'twixt ease
Of talk and sweet long silences,
    She stood among the plants in bloom
    At windows of a summer room,
To feign the shadow of the trees.

And as I wrought, while all above
    And all around was fragrant air,
In the sick burthen of my love
    It seemed each sun-thrilled blossom there
Beat like a heart among the leaves.
O heart that never beats nor heaves,
    In that one darkness lying still,

What now to thee my love's great will
Or the fine web the sunshine weaves?

For now doth daylight disavow
   Those days—nought left to see or hear.
Only in solemn whispers now
   At night-time these things reach mine ear;
When the leaf-shadows at a breath
Shrink in the road, and all the heath,
   Forest and water, far and wide,
   In limpid starlight glorified,
Lie like the mystery of death.

Last night at last I could have slept,
   And yet delayed my sleep till dawn,
Still wandering. Then it was I wept:
   For unawares I came upon
Those glades where once she walked with me:
And as I stood there suddenly,
   All wan with traversing the night,
   Upon the desolate verge of light
Yearned loud the iron-bosomed sea.

Even so, where Heaven holds breath and hears
   The beating heart of Love's own breast,—
Where round the secret of all spheres
   All angels lay their wings to rest,—
How shall my soul stand rapt and awed,
When, by the new birth borne abroad
   Throughout the music of the suns,
   It enters in her soul at once
And knows the silence there for God!

Here with her face doth memory sit
   Meanwhile, and wait the day's decline,
Till other eyes shall look from it,
   Eyes of the spirit's Palestine,
Even than the old gaze tenderer:
While hopes and aims long lost with her
   Stand round her image side by side,
   Like tombs of pilgrims that have died
About the Holy Sepulchre.

For Our Lady of the Rocks

BY LEONARDO DA VINCI

Mother, is this the darkness of the end,
   The Shadow of Death? and is that outer sea
   Infinite imminent Eternity?
And does the death-pang by man's seed sustained
In Time's each instant cause thy face to bend
   Its silent prayer upon the Son, while He
   Blesses the dead with His hand silently
To His long day which hours no more offend?

Mother of grace, the pass is difficult,
   Keen as these rocks, and the bewildered souls
     Throng it like echoes, blindly shuddering through.
   Thy name, O Lord, each spirit's voice extols,
     Whose peace abides in the dark avenue
Amid the bitterness of things occult.

At the Sun-rise in 1848

God said, Let there be light; and there was light.
    Then heard we sounds as though the Earth did sing
    And the Earth's angel cried upon the wing:
We saw priests fall together and turn white:
And covered in the dust from the sun's sight,
    A king was spied, and yet another king.
    We said: "The round world keeps its balancing;
On this globe, they and we are opposite,—
If it is day with us, with them 'tis night."
    Still, Man, in thy just pride, remember this:—
        Thou hadst not made that thy sons' sons shall ask
        What the word *king* may mean in their day's task,
    But for the light that led: and if light is,
It is because God said, Let there be light.

A Trip to Paris and Belgium

I

LONDON TO FOLKESTONE
(Half-past one to half-past five)

A constant keeping-past of shaken trees,
And a bewildered glitter of loose road;
Banks of bright growth, with single blades atop
Against white sky; and wires—a constant chain—
That seem to draw the clouds along with them
(Things which one stoops against the light to see
Through the low window; shaking by at rest,
Or fierce like water as the swiftness grows);
And, seen through fences or a bridge far off,
Trees that in moving keep their intervals

Still one 'twixt bar and bar; and then at times
Long reaches of green level, where one cow,
Feeding among her fellows that feed on,
Lifts her slow neck, and gazes for the sound.

There are six of us: I that write away;
Hunt reads Dumas, hard-lipped, with heavy jowl
And brows hung low, and the long ends of hair
Standing out limp. A grazier at one end
(Thank luck not my end!) has blocked out the air,
And sits in heavy consciousness of guilt.
The poor young muff who's face to face with me
Is pitiful in loose collar and black tie,
His latchet-button shaking as we go.
There are flowers by me, half upon my knees,
Owned by a dame who's fair in soul, no doubt:
The wind that beats among us carries off
Their scent, but still I have them for my eye.

Fields mown in ridges; and close garden-crops
Of the earth's increase; and a constant sky
Still with clear trees that let you see the wind;
And snatches of the engine-smoke, by fits
Tossed to the wind against the landscape, where
Rooks stooping heave their wings upon the day.

Brick walls we pass between, passed so at once
That for the suddenness I cannot know
Or what, or where begun, or where at end.
Sometimes a Station in grey quiet; whence,
With a short gathered champing of pent sound,
We are let out upon the air again.
Now nearly darkness; knees and arms and sides
Feel the least touch, and close about the face

A wind of noise that is along like God.
Pauses of water soon, at intervals,
That has the sky in it;—the reflexes
O' the trees move towards the bank as we go by,
Leaving the water's surface plain. I now
Lie back and close my eyes a space; for they
Smart from the open forwardness of thought
Fronting the wind—

       —I did not scribble more,
Be certain, after this; but yawned, and read,
And nearly dozed a little, I believe;
Till, stretching up against the carriage-back,
I was roused altogether, and looked out
To where, upon the desolate verge of light,
Yearned, pale and vast, the iron-coloured sea.

II

BOULOGNE TO AMIENS AND PARIS

(*3 to 11 p.m.; 3rd class*)

Strong extreme speed, that the brain hurries with,
Further than trees, and hedges, and green grass
Whitened by distance,—further than small pools
Held among fields and gardens,—further than
Haystacks and windmill-sails and roofs and herds,—
The sea's last margin ceases at the sun.

The sea has left us, but the sun remains.
Sometimes the country spreads aloof in tracts
Smooth from the harvest; sometimes sky and land
Are shut from the square space the window leaves
By a dense crowd of trees, stem behind stem

Passing across each other as we pass:
Sometimes tall poplar-wands stand white, their heads
Outmeasuring the distant hills. Sometimes
The ground has a deep greenness; sometimes brown
In stubble; and sometimes no ground at all,
For the close strength of crops that stand unreaped.
The water-plots are sometimes all the sun's,—
Sometimes quite green through shadows filling them,
Or islanded with growths of reeds,—or else
Masked in grey dust like the wide face o' the fields.
And still the swiftness lasts; that to our speed
The trees seem shaken like a press of spears.

There is some count of us:—folks travelling-capped,
Priesthood, and lank hard-featured soldiery,
Females (no women), blouses, Hunt, and I.

We are relayed at Amiens. The steam
Snorts, chafes, and bridles, like three-hundred horse,
And flings its dusky mane upon the air.
Our company is thinned, and lamps alight:
But still there are the folks in travelling-caps—
No priesthood now, but always soldiery,
And babies to make up for show in noise,
Females (no women), blouses, Hunt, and I.

Our windows at one side are shut for warmth;
Upon the other side, a leaden sky,
Hung in blank glare, makes all the country dim,
Which too seems bald and meagre,—be it truth,
Or of the waxing darkness. Here and there
The shade takes light, where in thin patches stand
The unstirred dregs of water.
                                        Hunt can see

A moon, he says; but I am too far back.
Still the same speed and thunder. We are stopped
Again, and speech tells clearer than in day.

Hunt has just stretched to tell me that he fears
I and my note-book may be taken for
The stuff that goes to make an "émissaire
De la perfide." Let me abate my zeal:
There is a stout gendarme within the coach.

This cursed pitching is too bad. My teeth
Jingle together in it; and my legs
(Which I got wet at Boulogne this good day
Wading for star-fish) are so chilled that I
Would don my coat, were not these seats too hard
To spare it from beneath me, and were not
The love of ease less than the love of sloth.

Hunt has just told me it is nearly eight:
We do not reach till half-past ten. Drat verse,
And steam, and Paris, and the fins of Time!
Marry, for me, look you, I will go sleep.

Most of them slept; I could not—held awake
By jolting clamour, with shut eyes; my head
Willing to nod and fancy itself vague.
Only at Stations I looked round me, when
Short silence paused among us, and I felt
A creeping in my feet from abrupt calm.
At such times Hunt would jerk himself, and then
Tumble uncouthly forward in his sleep.
This lasted near three hours. The darkness now
Stayeth behind us on the sullen road,
And all this light is Paris. Dieu merci.

Send me, dear William, by return of post,
As much as you can manage of that rhyme
Incurred at Ventnor. Bothers and delays
Have still prevented me from copying this
Till now; now that I do so, let it be
Anticipative compensation.
Numéro 4 Rue Geoffroy Marie,
Faubourg Montmartre, près des Boulevards.
Dear William, labelled thus the thing will reach.

III
THE STAIRCASE OF NOTRE DAME, PARIS

As one who, groping in a narrow stair,
   Hath a strong sound of bells upon his ears,
   Which, being at a distance off, appears
Quite close to him because of the pent air:
So with this France. She stumbles file and square
   Darkling and without space for breath: each one
   Who hears the thunder says: "It shall soon
Be in among her ranks to scatter her."

This may be; and it may be that the storm
   Is spent in rain upon the unscathed seas,
     Or wasteth other countries ere it die:
Till she,—having climbed always through the swarm
   Of darkness and of hurtling sound,—from these
     Shall step forth on the light in a still sky.

IV

PLACE DE LA BASTILLE, PARIS

How dear the sky has been above this place!
    Small treasures of this sky that we see here
    Seen weak through prison-bars from year to year;
Eyed with a painful prayer upon God's grace
To save, and tears which stayed along the face
    Lifted at sunset. Yea, how passing dear
    Those nights when through the bars a wind left clear
The heaven, and moonlight soothed the limpid space!

So was it, till one night the secret kept
    Safe in low vault and stealthy corridor
        Was blown abroad on gospel-tongues of flame.
O ways of God, mysterious evermore!
How many on this spot have cursed and wept
        That all might stand here now and own Thy Name.

V

ON A HANDFUL OF FRENCH MONEY

These coins that jostle on my hand do own
    No single image: each name here and date
    Denoting in man's consciousness and state
New change. In some, the face is clearly known,—
In others marred. The badge of that old throne
    Of Kings is on the obverse; or this sign
    Which says, "I France am all—lo, I am mine!"
Or else the Eagle that dared soar alone.
Even as these coins, so are these lives and years
    Mixed and bewildered; yet hath each of them
        No less its part in what is come to be

For France. Empire, Republic, Monarchy,—
   Each clamours or keeps silence in her name,
And lives within the pulse that now is hers.

VI
TO THE P.R.B.

Woolner and Stephens, Collinson, Millais,
   And my first brother, each and every one,
    What portion is theirs now beneath the sun
Which, even as here, in England makes to-day?
For most of them life runs not the same way
   Always, but leaves the thought at loss: I know
    Merely that Woolner keeps not even the show
Of work, nor is enough awake for play.
Meanwhile Hunt and myself race at full speed
   Along the Louvre, and yawn from school to school,
    Wishing worn-out those masters known as old.
And no man asks of Browning; though indeed
   (As the book travels with me) any fool
    Who would might hear Sordello's story told.

VII
IN THE TRAIN, AND AT VERSAILLES

In a dull swiftness we are carried by
   With bodies left at sway and shaking knees.
   The wind has ceased, or is a feeble breeze
Warm in the sun. The leaves are not yet dry
From yesterday's dense rain. All, low and high,
   A strong green country; but, among its trees,
   Ruddy and thin with Autumn. After these
There is the city still before the sky.

Versailles is reached. Pass we the galleries
  And seek the gardens. A great silence here,
    Through the long planted alleys, to the long
    Distance of water. More than tune or song,
Silence shall grow to awe within thine eyes,
  Till thy thought swim with the blue turning sphere.

VIII

LAST VISIT TO THE LOUVRE

The Cry of the P.R.B.,
after a careful examination of the canvases
of Rubens, Correggio, et hoc genus omne.

Non noi pittori! God of Nature's truth,
  If these, not we! Be it not said, when one
  Of us goes hence: "As these did, he hath done;
His feet sought out their footprints from his youth."
Because, dear God! the flesh Thou madest smooth
  These carked and fretted, that it seemed to run
  With ulcers; and the daylight of thy sun
They parcelled into blots and glares, uncouth
With stagnant grouts of paint. Men say that these
  Had further sight than man's, but that God saw
    Their works were good. God that didst know them foul!
    In such a blindness, blinder than the owl,
Leave us! Our sight can reach unto thy seas
  And hills; and 'tis enough for tears of awe.

IX

LAST SONNETS AT PARIS

I

Chins that might serve the new Jerusalem;
   Streets footsore; minute whisking milliners
   Dubbed graceful, but at whom one's eye demurs,
Knowing of England; ladies, much the same;
Bland smiling dogs with manes—a few of them
   At pains to look like sporting characters;
   Vast humming tabbies smothered in their furs;
Groseille, orgeat, meringues à la crême—
Good things to study; ditto bad—the maps
   Of sloshy colour in the Louvre; *cinq-francs*
   The largest coin; and at the restaurants
Large Ibrahim Pachas in Turkish caps
   To pocket them. *Un million d'habitants:*
Cast up, they'll make an Englishman—perhaps.

II

Tiled floors in bedrooms; trees (now run to seed—
   Such seed as the wind takes) of Liberty;
   Squares with new names that no one seems to see;
Scrambling Briarean passages, which lead
To the first place you came from; urgent need
   Of unperturbed nasal philosophy;
   Through Paris (what with church and gallery)
Some forty first-rate paintings,—or indeed
Fifty mayhap; fine churches; splendid inns;
   Fierce sentinels (toy-size without the stands)
     Who spit their oaths at you and grind their r's
If at a fountain you would wash your hands;
     One Frenchman (this is fact) who thinks he spars:—
Can even good dinners cover all these sins?

III

Yet in the mighty French metropolis
   Our time has not gone from us utterly
   In waste. The wise man saith, "An ample fee
For toil, to work thine end." Aye that it is.
Should England ask, "Was narrow prejudice
   Stretched to its utmost point unflinchingly,
   Even unto lying, at all times, by ye?"
We can say firmly: "Lord, thou knowest this,
Our soil may own us." Having but small French,
   Hunt passed for a stern Spartan all the while,
      Uncompromising, of few words: for me—
      I think I was accounted generally
   A fool, and just a little cracked. Thy smile
May light on us, Britannia, healthy wench.

X

FROM PARIS TO BRUSSELS
(*11 P.M. 15 October to half-past 1 P.M. 16*)

PROEM AT THE PARIS STATION

In France (to baffle thieves and murderers)
A journey takes two days of passport work
At least. The plan's sometimes a tedious one,
But bears its fruit. Because, the other day,
In passing by the Morgue, we saw a man
(The thing is common, and we never should
Have known of it, only we passed that way)
Who had been stabbed and tumbled in the Seine,
Where he had stayed some days. The face was black,
And, like a negro's, swollen; all the flesh
Had furred, and broken into a green mould.

Now, very likely, he who did the job
Was standing among those who stood with us,
To look upon the corpse. You fancy him—
Smoking an early pipe, and watching, as
An artist, the effect of his last work.
This always if it had not struck him that
'Twere best to leave while yet the body took
Its crust of rot beneath the Seine. It may:
But, if it did not, he can now remain
Without much fear. *Only,* if he should want
To travel, and have not his passport yet,
(Deep dogs these French police!) he may be caught.

Therefore you see (lest, being murderers,
We should not have the sense to go before
The thing were known, or to stay afterwards)
There is good reason why—having resolved
To start for Belgium—we were kept three days
To learn about the passports first, then do
As we had learned. This notwithstanding, in
The fullness of the time 'tis come to pass.

XI

ON THE ROAD

October, and eleven after dark:
Both mist and night. Among us in the coach
Packed heat on which the windows have been shut:
Our backs unto the motion—Hunt's and mine.
The last lamps of the Paris Station move
Slow with wide haloes past the clouded pane;
The road in secret empty darkness. One
Who sits beside me, now I turn, has pulled

A nightcap to his eyes. A woman here,
Knees to my knees—a twenty-nine-year-old—
Smiles at the mouth I open, seeing him:
I look her gravely in the jaws, and write.
Already while I write heads have been leaned
Upon the wall,—the lamp that's overhead
Dropping its shadow to the waist and hands.

Some time 'twixt sleep and wake. A dead pause then,
With giddy humming silence in the ears.
It is a Station. Eyes are opening now,
And mouths collecting their propriety.
From one of our two windows, now drawn up,
A lady leans, hawks a clear throat, and spits.

Hunt lifts his head from my cramped shoulder where
It has been lying—long stray hairs from it
Crawling upon my face and teazing me.
Ten minutes' law. Our feet are in the road.
A weak thin dimness at the sky, whose chill
Lies vague and hard. The mist of crimson heat
Hangs, a spread glare, about our engine's bulk.
I shall get in again, and sleep this time.

A heavy clamour that fills up the brain
Like thought grown burdensome; and in the ears
Speed that seems striving to o'ertake itself;
And in the pulses torpid life, which shakes
As water to a stir of wind beneath.

Poor Hunt, who has the toothache and can't smoke,
Has asked me twice for brandy. I would sleep;
But man proposes, and no more. I sit
With open eyes, and a head quite awake,

But which keeps catching itself lolled aside
And looking sentimental. In the coach,
If any one tries talking, the voice jolts,
And stuns the ear that stoops for it.

Amiens.

Half-an-hour's rest. Another shivering walk
Along the station, waiting for the bell.
Ding-dong. Now this time, by the Lord, I'll sleep.

I must have slept some while. Now that I wake,
Day is beginning in a kind of haze
White with grey trees. The hours have had their lapse.
A sky too dull for cloud. A country lain
In fields, where teams drag up the furrow yet;
Or else a level of trees, the furthest ones
Seen like faint clouds at the horizon's point.
Quite a clear distance, though in vapour. Mills
That turn with the dry wind. Large stacks of hay
Made to look bleak. Dead autumn, and no sun.

The smoke upon our course is borne so near
Along the earth, the earth appears to steam.
Blanc-Misseron, the last French station, passed.
We are in Belgium. It is just the same:—
Nothing to write of, and no good in verse.

Curse the big mounds of sand-weed! curse the miles
Of barren chill,—the twentyfold relays!
Curse every beastly Station on the road!

As well to write as swear. Hunt was just now
Making great eyes because outside the pane
One of the stokers passed whom he declared

A stunner. A vile mummy with a bag
Is squatted next me: a disgusting girl
Broad opposite. We have a poet, though,
Who is a gentleman, and looks like one;
Only he seems ashamed of writing verse,
And heads each new page with *"Mon cher Ami."*
Hunt's stunner has just come into the coach,
And set us hard agrin from ear to ear.

Another Station. There's a stupid horn
Set wheezing. Now I should just like to know
—Just merely for the whim—what good that is.
These Stations for the most part are a kind
Of London coal-merchant's back premises;
Whitewashed, but as by hands of coal-heavers;
Grimy themselves, and always circled in
With foul coke-loads that make the nose aroint.

Here is a Belgian village,—no, a town
Moated and buttressed. Next, a water-track
Lying with draggled reeds in a flat slime.
Next, the old country, always all the same.
Now by Hans Hemmling and by John Van Eyck,
You'll find, till something's new, I write no more.

                    (4 hours)

There is small change of country; but the sun
Is out, and it seems shame this were not said:
For upon all the grass the warmth has caught;
And betwixt distant whitened poplar-stems
Makes greener darkness; and in dells of trees
Shows spaces of a verdure that was hid;
And the sky has its blue floated with white,

And crossed with falls of the sun's glory aslant
To lay upon the waters of the world;
And from the road men stand with shaded eyes
To look; and flowers in gardens have grown strong,
And our own shadows here within the coach
Are brighter; and all colour has more bloom.

So, after the sore torments of the route:—
Toothache, and headache, and the ache of wind,
And huddled sleep, and smarting wakefulness,
And night, and day, and hunger sick at food,
And twentyfold relays, and packages
To be unlocked, and passports to be found,
And heavy well-kept landscape;—we were glad
Because we entered Brussels in the sun.

XII

ON THE ROAD TO WATERLOO: 17 OCTOBER
(En vigilante, 2 hours)

It is grey tingling azure overhead
    With silver drift. Beneath, where from the green
    The trees are reared, the distance stands between
At peace: and on this side the whole is spread
For sowing and for harvest, subjected
    Clear to the sky and wind. The sun's slow height
    Holds it through noon, and at the furthest night
It lies to the moist starshine and is fed.
Sometimes there is no country seen (for miles
    You think) because of the near roadside path
        Dense with long forest. Where the waters run
    They have the sky sunk into them—a bath
Of still blue heat; and in their flow, at whiles,
        There is a blinding vortex of the sun.

XIII
A HALF-WAY PAUSE

The turn of noontide has begun.
   In the weak breeze the sunshine yields.
   There is a bell upon the fields.
On the long hedgerow's tangled run
   A low white cottage intervenes:
   Against the wall a blind man leans,
And sways his face to have the sun.

Our horses' hoofs stir in the road,
   Quiet and sharp. Light hath a song
   Whose silence, being heard, seems long.
The point of noon maketh abode,
   And will not be at once gone through.
   The sky's deep colour saddens you,
And the heat weighs a dreamy load.

XIV
ON THE FIELD OF WATERLOO

So then, the name which travels side by side
   With English life from childhood—Waterloo—
   Means this. The sun is setting. "Their strife grew
Till the sunset, and ended," says our guide.
It lacked the "chord" by stage-use sanctified,
   Yet I believe one should have thrilled. For me,
   I grinned not, and 'twas something;—certainly
These held their point, and did not turn but died:

132 | THE ESSENTIAL ROSSETTI

So much is very well. "Under each span
  Of these ploughed fields" ('tis the guide still) "there rot
    Three nations' slain, a thousand-thousandfold."
      Am I to weep? Good sirs, the earth is old:
  Of the whole earth there is no single spot
But hath among its dust the dust of man.

XV
RETURNING TO BRUSSELS

Upon a Flemish road, when noon was deep,
  I passed a little consecrated shrine,
    Where, among simple pictures ranged in line,
The blessed Mary holds her child asleep.
To kneel here, shepherd-maidens leave their sheep
  When they feel grave because of the sunshine,
    And again kneel here in the day's decline;
And here, when their life ails them, come to weep.
Night being full, I passed on the same road
  By the same shrine; within, a lamp was lit
Which through the silence of clear darkness glowed.
    Thus, when life's heat is past and doubts arise
  Darkling, the lamp of Faith must strengthen it,
    Which sometimes will not light and sometimes dies.

XVI
ANTWERP TO GHENT

  We are upon the Scheldt. We know we move
Because there is a floating at our eyes
Whatso they seek; and because all the things
Which on our outset were distinct and large

Are smaller and much weaker and quite grey,
And at last gone from us. No motion else.

We are upon the road. The thin swift moon
Runs with the running clouds that are the sky,
And with the running water runs—at whiles
Weak 'neath the film and heavy growth of reeds.
The country swims with motion. Time itself
Is consciously beside us, and perceived.
Our speed is such the sparks our engine leaves
Are burning after the whole train has passed.

The darkness is a tumult. We tear on,
The roll behind us and the cry before,
Constantly, in a lull of intense speed
And thunder. Any other sound is known
Merely by sight. The shrubs, the trees your eye
Scans for their growth, are far along in haze.
The sky has lost its clouds, and lies away
Oppressively at calm: the moon has failed:
Our speed has set the wind against us. Now
Our engine's heat is fiercer, and flings up
Great glares alongside. Wind and steam and speed
And clamour and the night. We are in Ghent.

XVII

ANTWERP AND BRUGES

I climbed the stair in Antwerp church,
    What time the circling thews of sound
    At sunset seem to heave it round.
Far up, the carillon did search
The wind, and the birds came to perch
    Far under, where the gables wound.

In Antwerp harbour on the Scheldt
   I stood along, a certain space
   Of night. The mist was near my face;
Deep on, the flow was heard and felt.
The carillon kept pause, and dwelt
   In music through the silent place.

John Memmeling and John van Eyck
   Hold state at Bruges. In sore shame
   I scanned the works that keep their name.
The carillon, which then did strike
Mine ears, was heard of theirs alike:
   It set me closer unto them.

I climbed at Bruges all the flight
   The belfry has of ancient stone.
   For leagues I saw the east wind blown;
The earth was grey, the sky was white.
I stood so near upon the height
   That my flesh felt the carillon.

XVIII
ON LEAVING BRUGES

The city's steeple-towers remove away,
   Each singly; as each vain infatuate Faith
   Leaves God in heaven, and passes. A mere breath
Each soon appears, so far. Yet that which lay
The first is now scarce further or more grey
   Than the last is. Now all are wholly gone.
   The sunless sky has not once had the sun
Since the first weak beginning of the day.

The air falls back as the wind finishes,
   And the clouds stagnate. On the water's face
      The current breathes along, but is not stirred.
      There is no branch that thrills with any bird.
   Winter is to possess the earth a space,
And have its will upon the extreme seas.

XIX
ASHORE AT DOVER

On landing, the first voice one hears is from
   An English police-constable; a man
   Respectful, conscious that at need he can
Enforce respect. Our custom-house at home
Strict too, but quiet. Not the foul-mouthed scum
   Of passport-mongers who in Paris still
   Preserve the Reign of Terror; not the till
Where the King haggles, all through Belgium.
The country somehow seems in earnest here,
   Grave and sufficient:—*England,* so to speak;
No other word will make the thing as clear.
     "Ah! habit," you exclaim, "and prejudice!"
If so, so be it. One don't care to shriek,
     "Sir, this *shall be!*" But one believes it is.

For a Venetian Pastoral

BY GIORGIONE

(*In the Louvre*)

Water, for anguish of the solstice:—nay,
  But dip the vessel slowly,—nay, but lean
  And hark how at its verge the wave sighs in
Reluctant. Hush! beyond all depth away
The heat lies silent at the brink of day:
  Now the hand trails upon the viol-string
  That sobs, and the brown faces cease to sing,
Sad with the whole of pleasure. Whither stray
Her eyes now, from whose mouth the slim pipes creep
  And leave it pouting, while the shadowed grass
    Is cool against her naked side? Let be:—
Say nothing now unto her lest she weep,
  Nor name this ever. Be it as it was,—
    Life touching lips with Immortality.

For an Allegorical Dance of Women

BY ANDREA MANTEGNA

(*In the Louvre*)

Scarcely, I think; yet it indeed *may* be
  The meaning reached him, when this music rang
  Clear through his frame, a sweet possessive pang,
And he beheld these rocks and that ridged sea.
But I believe that, leaning tow'rds them, he
  Just felt their hair carried across his face
  As each girl passed him; nor gave ear to trace
How many feet; nor bent assuredly

His eyes from the blind fixedness of thought
  To know the dancers. It is bitter glad
    Even unto tears. Its meaning filleth it,
      A secret of the wells of Life: to wit:—
  The heart's each pulse shall keep the sense it had
With all, though the mind's labour run to nought.

For "Ruggiero and Angelica"

BY INGRES

I

A remote sky, prolonged to the sea's brim:
  One rock-point standing buffeted alone,
    Vexed at its base with a foul beast unknown,
Hell-birth of geomaunt and teraphim:
A knight, and a winged creature bearing him,
  Reared at the rock: a woman fettered there,
    Leaning into the hollow with loose hair
And throat let back and heartsick trail of limb.

The sky is harsh, and the sea shrewd and salt:
  Under his lord the griffin-horse ramps blind
    With rigid wings and tail. The spear's lithe stem
  Thrills in the roaring of those jaws: behind,
That evil length of body chafes at fault.
    She does not hear nor see—she knows of them.

II

Clench thine eyes now,—'tis the last instant, girl:
   Draw in thy senses, set thy knees, and take
   One breath for all: thy life is keen awake,—
Thou mayst not swoon. Was that the scattered whirl
Of its foam drenched thee?—or the waves that curl
   And split, bleak spray wherein thy temples ache?
   Or was it his champion's blood to flake
Thy flesh?—or thine own blood's anointing, girl?

Now, silence: for the sea's is such a sound
   As irks not silence; and except the sea,
      All now is still. Now the dead thing doth cease
To writhe, and drifts. He turns to her: and she,
Cast from the jaws of Death, remains there, bound,
      Again a woman in her nakedness.

For a Virgin and Child

BY HANS MEMMELINCK
(*In the Academy of Bruges*)

Mystery: God, man's life born into man
   Of woman. There abideth on her brow
   The ended pang of knowledge, the which now
Is calm assured. Since first her task began
She hath known all. What more of anguish than
   Endurance oft hath lived through, the whole space
   Through night till day, passed weak upon her face
While the heard lapse of darkness slowly ran?

All hath been told her touching her dear Son,
　And all shall be accomplished. Where He sits
　　Even now, a babe, He holds the symbol fruit
Perfect and chosen. Until God permits,
　　His soul's elect still have the absolute
Harsh nether darkness, and make painful moan.

For a Marriage of St. Catherine

BY THE SAME
(*In the Hospital of St. John at Bruges*)

Mystery: Catherine the bride of Christ.
　She kneels, and on her hand the holy Child
　　Now sets the ring. Her life is hushed and mild,
Laid in God's knowledge—ever unenticed
From God, and in the end thus fitly priced.
　　Awe, and the music that is near her, wrought
　　Of angels, have possessed her eyes in thought:
Her utter joy is hers, and hath sufficed.

There is a pause while Mary Virgin turns
　The leaf, and reads. With eyes on the spread book,
　　That damsel at her knees reads after her.
　　John whom He loved, and John His harbinger,
　Listen and watch. Whereon soe'er thou look,
The light is starred in gems and the gold burns.

The Sea-Limits

Consider the sea's listless chime:
   Time's self it is, made audible,—
   The murmur of the earth's own shell.
Secret continuance sublime
   Is the sea's end: our sight may pass
   No furlong further. Since time was,
This sound hath told the lapse of time.

No quiet, which is death's,—it hath
   The mournfulness of ancient life,
   Enduring always at dull strife.
As the world's heart of rest and wrath,
   Its painful pulse is in the sands.
   Last utterly, the whole sky stands,
Grey and not known, along its path.

Listen alone beside the sea,
   Listen alone among the woods;
   Those voices of twin solitudes
Shall have one sound alike to thee:
   Hark where the murmurs of thronged men
   Surge and sink back and surge again,—
Still the one voice of wave and tree.

Gather a shell from the strown beach
   And listen at its lips: they sigh
   The same desire and mystery,
The echo of the whole sea's speech.
   And all mankind is thus at heart
   Not anything but what thou art:
And Earth, Sea, Man, are all in each.

The Mirror

She knew it not:—most perfect pain
　　To learn: this too she knew not. Strife
　　　　For me, calm hers, as from the first.
　　　　'Twas but another bubble burst
　　Upon the curdling draught of life,—
My silent patience mine again.

As who, of forms that crowd unknown
　　Within a distant mirror's shade,
　　　　Deems such an one himself, and makes
　　　　Some sign; but when the image shakes
　　No whit, he finds his thought betray'd,
And must seek elsewhere for his own.

During Music

O cool unto the sense of pain
　　That last night's sleep could not destroy;
　　O warm unto the sense of joy,
That dreams its life within the brain.

What though I lean o'er thee to scan
　　The written music cramped and stiff;—
　　'Tis dark to me, as hieroglyph
On those weird bulks Egyptian.

But as from those, dumb now, and strange,
　　A glory wanders on the earth,
　　Even so thy tones can call a birth
From these, to shake my soul with change.

O swift, as in melodious haste
   Float o'er the keys thy fingers small;
   O soft, as is the rise and fall
Which stirs that shade within thy breast.

Penumbra

I did not look upon her eyes,
(Though scarcely seen, with no surprise,
'Mid many eyes a single look,)
Because they should not gaze rebuke,
At night, from stars in sky and brook.

I did not take her by the hand,
(Though little was to understand
From touch of hand all friends might take,)
Because it should not prove a flake
Burnt in my palm to boil and ache.

I did not listen to her voice,
(Though none had noted, where at choice
All might rejoice in listening,)
Because no such a thing should cling
In the wood's moan at evening.

I did not cross her shadow once,
(Though from the hollow west the sun's
Last shadow runs along so far,)
Because in June it should not bar
My ways, at noon when fevers are.

They told me she was sad that day,
(Though wherefore tell what love's soothsay,
Sooner than they, did register?)
And my heart leapt and wept to her,
And yet I did not speak nor stir.

So shall the tongues of the sea's foam
(Though many voices therewith come
From drowned hope's home to cry to me,)
Bewail one hour the more, when sea
And wind are one with memory.

Words on the Window-pane*

Did she in summer write it, or in spring,
    Or with this wail of autumn at her ears,
    Or in some winter left among old years
Scratched it through tettered cark? A certain thing
That round her heart the frost was hardening,
    Not to be thawed of tears, which on this pane
    Channelled the rime, perchance, in fevered rain,
For false man's sake and love's most bitter sting.

Howbeit, between this last word and the next
    Unwritten, subtly seasoned was the smart,
        And here at least the grace to weep: if she,
Rather, midway in her disconsolate text,
    Rebelled not, loathing from the trodden heart
        That thing which she had found man's love to be.

*For a woman's fragmentary inscription.

A Match with the Moon

Weary already, weary miles to-night
   I walked for bed: and so, to get some ease,
   I dogged the flying moon with similes.
And like a wisp she doubled on my sight
In ponds; and caught in tree-tops like a kite;
   And in a globe of film all liquorish
   Swam full-faced like a silly silver fish;—
Last like a bubble shot the welkin's height
Where my road turned, and got behind me, and sent
   My wizened shadow craning round at me,
   And jeered, "So, step the measure,—one two three!"
And if I faced on her, looked innocent.
But just at parting, halfway down a dell,
She kissed me for good-night. So you'll not tell.

Sudden Light

   I have been here before,
      But when or how I cannot tell:
   I know the grass beyond the door,
      The sweet, keen smell,
The sighing sound, the lights around the shore.

   You have been mine before,—
      How long ago I may not know:
   But just when at that swallow's soar
      Your neck turned so,
Some veil did fall,—I knew it all of yore.

   Has this been thus before?
      And shall not thus time's eddying flight

Still with our lives our love restore
        In death's despite,
And day and night yield one delight once more?

Dawn on the Night-Journey

Till dawn the wind drove round me. It is past
    And still, and leaves the air to lisp of bird,
    And to the quiet that is almost heard
Of the new-risen day, as yet bound fast
In the first warmth of sunrise. When the last
    Of the sun's hours to-day shall be fulfilled,
    There shall another breath of time be stilled
For me, which now is to my senses cast
As much beyond me as eternity,
    Unknown, kept secret. On the newborn air
    The moth quivers in silence. It is vast,
Yea, even beyond the hills upon the sea,
    The day whose end shall give this hour as sheer
        As chaos to the irrevocable Past.

The Woodspurge

The wind flapped loose, the wind was still,
Shaken out dead from tree and hill:
I had walked on at the wind's will,—
I sat now, for the wind was still.

Between my knees my forehead was,—
My lips, drawn in, said not Alas!
My hair was over in the grass,
My naked ears heard the day pass.

My eyes, wide open, had the run
Of some ten weeds to fix upon;
Among those few, out of the sun,
The woodspurge flowered, three cups in one.

From perfect grief there need not be
Wisdom or even memory:
One thing then learnt remains to me,—
The woodspurge has a cup of three.

Venus Verticordia

FOR A PICTURE

She hath the apple in her hand for thee,
    Yet almost in her heart would hold it back;
    She muses, with her eyes upon the track
Of that which in thy spirit they can see.
Haply, "Behold, he is at peace," saith she;
    "Alas! the apple for his lips,—the dart
    That follows its brief sweetness to his heart,—
The wandering of his feet perpetually!"

A little space her glance is still and coy;
    But if she give the fruit that works her spell,
Those eyes shall flame as for her Phrygian boy.
    Then shall her bird's strained throat the woe foretell,
    And her far seas moan as a single shell,
And through her dark grove strike the light of Troy.

A Sea-Spell

FOR A PICTURE

Her lute hangs shadowed in the apple-tree,
  While flashing fingers weave the sweet-strung spell
  Between its chords; and as the wild notes swell,
The sea-bird for those branches leaves the sea.
But to what sound her listening ear stoops she?
  What netherworld gulf-whispers doth she hear,
  In answering echoes from what planisphere,
Along the wind, along the estuary?

She sinks into her spell: and when full soon
  Her lips move and she soars into her song,
  What creatures of the midmost main shall throng
In furrowed surf-clouds to the summoning rune;
Till he, the fated mariner, hears her cry,
And up her rock, bare-breasted, comes to die?

Troy Town

Heavenborn Helen, Sparta's queen,
            (*O Troy Town!*)
Had two breasts of heavenly sheen,
The sun and moon of the heart's desire:
All Love's lordship lay between.
            (*O Troy's down,
            Tall Troy's on fire!*)

Helen knelt at Venus' shrine,
            (*O Troy Town!*)
Saying, "A little gift is mine,

A little gift for a heart's desire.
Hear me speak and make me a sign!
        (*O Troy's down,*
        Tall Troy's on fire!)

"Look, I bring thee a carven cup;
        (*O Troy Town!*)
See it here as I hold it up,—
Shaped it is to the heart's desire,
Fit to fill when the gods would sup.
        (*O Troy's down,*
        Tall Troy's on fire!)

"It was moulded like my breast;
        (*O Troy Town!*)
He that sees it may not rest,
Rest at all for his heart's desire.
O give ear to my heart's behest!
        (*O Troy's down,*
        Tall Troy's on fire!)

"See my breast, how like it is;
        (*O Troy Town!*)
See it bare for the air to kiss!
Is the cup to thy heart's desire?
O for the breast, O make it his!
        (*O Troy's down,*
        Tall Troy's on fire!)

"Yea, for my bosom here I sue;
        (*O Troy Town!*)
Thou must give it where 'tis due,
Give it there to the heart's desire.

Whom do I give my bosom to?
>>(*O Troy's down,*
>>*Tall Troy's on fire!*)

"Each twin breast is an apple sweet.
>>(*O Troy Town!*)
Once an apple stirred the beat
Of thy heart with the heart's desire:—
Say, who brought it then to thy feet?
>>(*O Troy's down,*
>>*Tall Troy's on fire!*)

"They that claimed it then were three:
>>(*O Troy Town!*)
For thy sake two hearts did he
Make forlorn of the heart's desire.
Do for him as he did for thee!
>>(*O Troy's down,*
>>*Tall Troy's on fire!*)

"Mine are apples grown to the south,
>>(*O Troy Town!*)
Grown to taste in the days of drouth,
Taste and waste to the heart's desire:
Mine are apples meet for his mouth."
>>(*O Troy's down,*
>>*Tall Troy's on fire!*)

Venus looked on Helen's gift,
>>(*O Troy Town!*)
Looked and smiled with subtle drift,
Saw the work of her heart's desire:—
"There thou kneel'st for Love to lift!"
>>(*O Troy's down,*
>>*Tall Troy's on fire!*)

Venus looked in Helen's face,
>   (*O Troy Town!*)
Knew far off an hour and place,
And fire lit from the heart's desire;
Laughed and said, "Thy gift hath grace!"
>   (*O Troy's down,*
>   *Tall Troy's on fire!*)

Cupid looked on Helen's breast,
>   (*O Troy Town!*)
Saw the heart within its nest,
Saw the flame of the heart's desire,—
Marked his arrow's burning crest.
>   (*O Troy's down,*
>   *Tall Troy's on fire!*)

Cupid took another dart,
>   (*O Troy Town!*)
Fledged it for another heart,
Winged the shaft with the heart's desire,
Drew the string and said, "Depart!"
>   (*O Troy's down,*
>   *Tall Troy's on fire!*)

Paris turned upon his bed,
>   (*O Troy Town!*)
Turned upon his bed and said,
Dead at heart with the heart's desire—
"Oh to clasp her golden head!"
>   (*O Troy's down,*
>   *Tall Troy's on fire!*)

A Death-Parting

Leaves and rain and the days of the year,
  (*Water-willow and wellaway,*)
All these fall, and my soul gives ear,
And she is hence who once was here.
  (*With a wind blown night and day.*)

Ah! but now, for a secret sign,
  (*The willow's wan and the water white,*)
In the held breath of the day's decline
Her very face seemed pressed to mine.
  (*With a wind blown day and night.*)

O love, of my death my life is fain;
  (*The willows wave on the water-way,*)
Your cheek and mine are cold in the rain,
But warm they'll be when we meet again.
  (*With a wind blown night and day.*)

Mists are heaved and cover the sky;
  (*The willows wail in the waning light,*)
O loose your lips, leave space for a sigh,—
They seal my soul, I cannot die.
  (*With a wind blown day and night.*)

Leaves and rain and the days of the year,
  (*Water-willow and wellaway,*)
All still fall, and I still give ear,
And she is hence, and I am here.
  (*With a wind blown night and day.*)

For Spring

BY SANDRO BOTTICELLI
(*In the Accademia of Florence*)

What masque of what old wind-withered New-Year
   Honours this Lady? Flora, wanton-eyed
   For birth, and with all flowrets prankt and pied:
Aurora, Zephyrus, with mutual cheer
Of clasp and kiss: the Graces circling near,
   'Neath bower-linked arch of white arms glorified:
   And with those feathered feet which hovering glide
O'er Spring's brief bloom, Hermes the harbinger.

Birth-bare, not death-bare yet, the young stems stand
   This Lady's temple-columns: o'er her head
   Love wings his shaft. What mystery here is read
Of homage or of hope? But how command
     Dead Springs to answer? And how question here
     These mummers of that wind-withered New-Year?

For the Holy Family

BY MICHELANGELO
(*In the National Gallery**)

Turn not the prophet's page, O Son! He knew
   All that Thou hast to suffer, and hath writ.
   Not yet Thine hour of knowledge. Infinite
The sorrows that Thy manhood's lot must rue

In this picture the Virgin Mother is seen withholding from the Child Saviour the prophetic writings in which His sufferings are foretold. Angelic figures beside them examine a scroll.

And dire acquaintance of Thy grief. That clue
   The spirits of Thy mournful ministerings
   Seek through yon scroll in silence. For these things
The angels have desired to look into.

Still before Eden waves the fiery sword,—
   Her Tree of Life unransomed: whose sad Tree
   Of Knowledge yet to growth of Calvary
      Must yield its Tempter,—Hell the earliest dead
Of Earth resign,—and yet, O Son and Lord,
      The seed o' the woman bruise the serpent's head.

"Found"

FOR A PICTURE

"There is a budding morrow in midnight:"—
   So sang our Keats, our English nightingale.
   And here, as lamps across the bridge turn pale
In London's smokeless resurrection-light,
Dark breaks to dawn. But o'er the deadly blight
   Of Love deflowered and sorrow of none avail,
   Which makes this man gasp and this woman quail,
Can day from darkness ever again take flight?

Ah! gave not these two hearts their mutual pledge,
Under one mantle sheltered 'neath the hedge
   In gloaming courtship? And, O God! to-day
      He only knows he holds her,—but what part
      Can life now take? She cries in her locked heart,—
   "Leave me—I do not know you—go away!"

The Orchard-Pit

Piled deep below the screening apple-branch
   They lie with bitter apples in their hands:
And some are only ancient bones that blanch,
And some had ships that last year's wind did launch,
   And some were yesterday the lords of lands.

In the soft dell, among the apple-trees,
   High up above the hidden pit she stands,
And there for ever sings, who gave to these,
That lie below, her magic hour of ease,
   And those her apples holden in their hands.

This in my dreams is shown me; and her hair
   Crosses my lips and draws my burning breath;
Her song spreads golden wings upon the air,
Life's eyes are gleaming from her forehead fair,
   And from her breasts the ravishing eyes of Death.

Men say to me that sleep hath many dreams,
   Yet I knew never but this dream alone:
There, from a dried-up channel, once the stream's,
The glen slopes up; even such in sleep it seems
   As to my waking sight the place well known.

◆ ◆

My love I call her, and she loves me well:
   But I love her as in the maelstrom's cup
The whirled stone loves the leaf inseparable
That clings to it round all the circling swell,
   And that the same last eddy swallows up.

TRANSLATIONS

Sestina

[DANTE ALIGHIERI]

Of the Lady Pietra degli Scrovigni

To the dim light and the large circle of shade
I have clomb, and to the whitening of the hills,
There where we see no colour in the grass.
Nathless my longing loses not its green,
It has so taken root in the hard stone
Which talks and hears as though it were a lady.

Utterly frozen is this youthful lady,
Even as the snow that lies within the shade;
For she is no more moved than is the stone
By the sweet season which makes warm the hills
And alters them afresh from white to green,
Covering their sides again with flowers and grass.

When on her hair she sets a crown of grass
The thought has no more room for other lady;
Because she weaves the yellow with the green
So well that Love sits down there in the shade,—
Love who has shut me in among low hills
Faster than between walls of granite-stone.

She is more bright than is a precious stone;
The wound she gives may not be healed with grass:
I therefore have fled far o'er plains and hills
For refuge from so dangerous a lady;

But from her sunshine nothing can give shade,—
Not any hill, nor wall, nor summer-green.

A while ago, I saw her dressed in green,—
So fair, she might have wakened in a stone
This love which I do feel even for her shade;
And therefore, as one woos a graceful lady,
I wooed her in a field that was all grass
Girdled about with very lofty hills.

Yet shall the streams turn back and climb the hills
Before Love's flame in this damp wood and green
Burn, as it burns within a youthful lady,
For my sake, who would sleep away in stone
My life, or feed like beasts upon the grass,
Only to see her garments cast a shade.

How dark soe'er the hills throw out their shade,
Under her summer-green the beautiful lady
Covers it, like a stone covered in grass.

The Ballad of Dead Ladies

[FRANÇOIS VILLON, 1450]

Tell me now in what hidden way is
    Lady Flora the lovely Roman?
Where's Hipparchia, and where is Thaïs,
    Neither of them the fairer woman?
    Where is Echo, beheld of no man,
Only heard on river and mere,—
    She whose beauty was more than human? . . .
But where are the snows of yester-year?

Where's Héloise, the learned nun,
    For whose sake Abeillard, I ween,
Lost manhood and put priesthood on?
    (From Love he won such dule and teen!)
    And where, I pray you, is the Queen
Who willed that Buridan should steer
    Sewed in a sack's mouth down the Seine? . . .
But where are the snows of yester-year?

White Queen blanche, like a queen of lilies,
    With a voice like any mermaiden,—
Bertha Broadfoot, Beatrice, Alice,
    And Ermengarde the lady of Maine,—
    And that good Joan whom Englishmen
At Rouen doomed and burned her there,—
    Mother of God, where are they then? . . .
But where are the snows of yester-year?

Nay, never ask this week, fair lord,
    Where they are gone, nor yet this year,
Save with thus much for an overword,—
    But where are the snows of yester-year?

About the Editor

❖❖

John Hollander was born in New York City on October 28, 1929, and educated in the New York City Public Schools and at Columbia. He was a Junior Fellow in the Harvard Society of Fellows and eventually got his Ph.D. from Indiana University. His first book of poems was selected for the Yale Series of Younger Poets by W. H. Auden in 1957, and he has since published eleven more books of poetry, including Reflections on Espionage, Spectral Emanations, Powers of Thirteen, In Time and Place, *and, most recently,* Harp Lake *(Knopf, 1988). Among his books of criticism are* Vision and Resonance, The Figure of Echo, *and* Melodious Guile. *He is also the author of* Rhyme's Reason, *a guide to English verse, and has edited nine volumes of verse and prose, including, with Frank Kermode,* The Oxford Anthology of English Literature. *Mr. Hollander has written books for children and has collaborated on operatic and lyric works with such composers as Milton Babbitt, George Perle, and Hugo Weisgall. He has taught at Hunter College and is now A. Bartlett Giamatti Professor of English at Yale University. He has won the Bollingen Prize for Poetry, the Levinson Prize, and Guggenheim and NEH fellowships, among others, and is a chancellor of the Academy of American Poets and a member both of the American Academy and Institute of Arts and Letters and of the American Academy of Arts and Sciences.*